MINNESOTA

DO YOUR OWN NONPROFIT

SECOND EDITION

MINNESOTA Do Your Own Nonprofit

Second Edition

Copyright © 2018 Regina Kitty Bickford. All Rights Reserved.

No rights claimed for public domain material, all rights reserved. No parts of this publication may be reproduced, stored in any retrieval system, or transmitted in any form or by any means, electronic, mechanical, recording, or otherwise, without the prior written permission of the author. Violations may be subject to civil or criminal penalties. If you have a need to reproduce this material, use it in a group educational or other settings, or wish to have the author speak to or assist your organization in the 501(c) (3) process, please contact author at the address below.

ISBN-13: 978-1-63308-306-6 (paperback journal edition)

Cover Design and Interior Design by *R'tor John D. Maghuyop*

1028 S Bishop Avenue, Dept. 178
Rolla, MO 65401

www.doyourownnonprofit.com
www.taxexempt501c3.com

Printed in the United States of America

MINNESOTA

DO YOUR OWN NONPROFIT

The ONLY GPS You Need for 501(c)(3) Tax Exempt Approval

SECOND EDITION

Dr. Kitty Bickford, DBS, CPC
FOUNDER: BENEVOLANCE AND PASTURE VALLEY CHILDREN MISSIONS

CHALFANT ECKERT
PUBLISHING

ALSO BY DR. KITTY BICKFORD:

This is book 23 of the **2nd Edition** of the 51-book *Do Your Own Nonprofit* state series.

Do Your Own Nonprofit 51-book state series

Nonprofit Touchdown:
Winning the 501(c) (3) Game Against IRS

To my wonderful husband, Jim, and my family and friends who support and encourage my efforts.

But above all, to Jesus my redeemer, savior, and friend who sticks closer than a brother, Father God who watches over me and protects me, and to the Holy Spirit who guides my path with His still small voice.

Thank You All!

TABLE OF CONTENTS

ACKNOWLEDGMENTS		9
DISCLAIMER		11
ABOUT THE AUTHOR		13

PART I	INITIAL ORGANIZATIONAL SETUP	17
Chapter 1	Pay Attention: I Am Only Gonna Say This Once!	19
Chapter 2	Myths About Nonprofits	21
Chapter 3	Is 501(c) (3) Status Right for You?	35
Chapter 4	Do-It-Yourself Checklist	45
Chapter 5	Select a Business Name and Make Sure It is Available	49
Chapter 6	Get a Federal Employer Identification Number (FEIN)	53
Chapter 7	Develop a Strong Mission Statement	63
Chapter 8	Form a Board of Directors	67
Chapter 9	Crash Course on Incorporation	79
Chapter 10	Let's Incorporate and Stay Compliant!	89
Chapter 11	Let's Create Bylaws	103
Chapter 12	Develop a Conflict of Interest Policy	133
Chapter 13	Hold and Document the First Board Meeting	145

PART II	IRS FORM 1023 APPLICATION FOR TAX-EXEMPT STATUS	149
Chapter 14	Request for Recognition of Exemption	151
Chapter 15	Part I: Identification of Applicant	157
Chapter 16	Part II: Organizational Structure	163
Chapter 17	Part III: Provisions in your Organizing Documents	167
Chapter 18	Part IV: Narrative Description of Your Activities	171
Chapter 19	Part V: Compensation and Other Financial Arrangements	175
Chapter 20	Part VI: Your Members and Others That Receive Benefits from You	183
Chapter 21	Part VII: Your History	187
Chapter 22	Part VIII: Specific Activities	189
Chapter 23	Part IX: Financial Data	203

Chapter 24	Part X: Public Charity Status	217
Chapter 25	Part XI: User Fee Information	221

PART III — IRS SCHEDULES FOR TAX-EXEMPT STATUS — 223

Chapter 26	Schedule A: Churches	225
Chapter 27	Schedule B: Schools, Colleges, and Universities	233
Chapter 28	Schedule C: Hospitals and Medical Research Organizations	239
Chapter 29	Schedule D: Section 509(a) (3) Supporting Organizations	245
Chapter 30	Schedule E: Organizations Not Filing Form 1023 Within 27 Months of Formation	251
Chapter 31	Schedule F: Homes for the Elderly or Handicapped and Low-Income Housing	255
Chapter 32	Schedule G: Successors to Other Organizations	259
Chapter 33	Schedule H: Organizations Providing Scholarships and Other Educational Support	261

PART IV — FORM 1023-EZ — 265

Chapter 34	Form 1023-EZ: Streamlined Application	267

PART V — SPECIAL FEATURE BY GRANT GURU JUDY HANNA — 273

Chapter 35	The Art of Grant Writing for Your Nonprofit	275

PART VI — SPECIAL CIRCUMSTANCES — 285

Chapter 36	Automatic Revocation of 501(c) (3) Status	287

PART VII — FOLLOW-UP TASKS — 291

Chapter 37	Annual Filing Requirements with IRS	293
Chapter 38	Apply for Nonprofit Standard Mail Rates	299

SUMMARY	301
APPENDIX A	303

ACKNOWLEDGMENTS

I serve a God who makes the impossible *totally* possible. In my own strength, I can do nothing, but I can do all things through Christ who strengthens me. My Christian walk has seen many twists and turns, each one more exciting than the last, and so much better than I could have dreamed up alone. Thank you, God, for your marvelous direction. Thank you, Holy Spirit, for that still small voice of guidance to keep me on the right path. Thank you, Jesus, for going to the cross in my stead so that I can have eternal life in heaven, and life abundantly in the meantime. It just doesn't get any better than that!

DISCLAIMER

While the information contained in this book was prepared with best efforts and in good faith, the publisher and author make no representations or warranties concerning the accuracy or completeness of the contents herein.

This work (in any electronic or digital form or any other printed material form) is not intended for use as a source of legal, accounting, tax, or financial advice. If advice concerning legal, accounting, tax, financial, or any other professional advice is needed, seek the services of a qualified, duly licensed, and competent professional.

The contents of this work reflect the views and opinions of the author. The author and publisher have made their best efforts to produce a high quality, informative, and helpful course on getting approved for Section 501(c) (3) status by the Internal Revenue Service (IRS). However, they make no representations or warranties of any kind about the completeness and accuracy of the contents of the course. Any slights of people and organizations are unintentional.

Neither the author nor the publisher accepts any liability of any kind for any losses or damages caused or alleged to be caused, directly or indirectly, from using the information contained in this book. Every individual must make his or her own decisions. Although this book describes the experiences of the author, it in no way guarantees similar successes for others. Every effort has been made to ensure that this publication is free from errors and problems.

ABOUT THE AUTHOR

Dr. Kitty Bickford lives, breathes, and eats nonprofits 24/6 (Sunday is the Lord's Day). She owns *Tax Exempt 501c3, LLC* and is an independent contractor for *Harbor Compliance*, both national incorporation services with great reputations and excellent services. She has completed over one thousand 501(c)(3) packages for IRS with no rejects, and contracts affordable follow-up consulting services to new nonprofits that need guidance for the first year as well as their first nonprofit tax return completed for them. Kitty is a Certified Professional Coach (CPC) for nonprofit business leaders and works with *Program to Aid Citizen Enterprise (PACE)* coaching nonprofit executives to grow their nonprofits.

MILITARY CAREER AND FAMILY

Dr. Kitty Bickford is a Christian woman who spent from 1979–1989 in the United States Air Force. The last five years of her military career were spent as a Master Instructor and On-the-Job Training Advisor for Air Training Command, achieving the noncommissioned officer rank of E-6 (Technical Sergeant).

In 1984, she met and eventually married Master Sergeant Jim Bickford, who was twenty-two years her senior. They have been happy together for over 30 years, enjoying four children, fourteen grandchildren (one with God), and two great-grandsons.

TEACHING AND MISSIONARY WORK

After leaving the military, Kitty continued her teaching career, first teaching college, then she retired from teaching public school. In 2006, Kitty was selected as ING Corporation's *Unsung Hero* for Missouri for educational innovation. She has made over 300 microfinance loans to the world's poor through Kiva.org, mostly disadvantaged women. These loans allow women to start their own businesses and become self-sufficient.

Kitty supports missionaries to Zimbabwe, Zambia, and Ukraine. She was awarded the 2013 Spirit of Rolla Award in recognition of significant achievement and/or lifetime contribution to the spirit of giving. She holds undergraduate degrees in Educational Administration, Behavioral Science, and Criminal Justice, completed the undergraduate teacher certification program for Missouri, holds a graduate degree in Psychology, has studied Special Education at the doctorate level, and holds a Doctorate in Biblical Studies.

PHILANTHROPY

In 2005, Kitty sponsored an orphaned child in Swaziland, Africa. When she went to visit him in 2012, she was disappointed to find that the organization she trusted to care for him lacked the integrity she expected. Upon returning to the United States, God led her to start a nonprofit organization that would not be corrupt and would actually do some good for hungry kids and vulnerable families.

Kitty soon found that the 501(c) (3) process was either long and complicated or very expensive. She chose the long and complicated option because spending up to $7,000 for an attorney to do paperwork seemed counterproductive. After much study, questioning, and hard work, IRS approved *Pasture Valley Children Missions* on the first try. Elated, she thanked God that the process was over so she could get down to work feeding children. To her surprise, God spoke to her spirit and told her to write a book for others who want to start a nonprofit on a shoestring. She wrote *Nonprofit Touchdown: Winning the 501(c) (3) Game Against IRS*. It was 370 pages long, a national edition that covered all 50 states and DC. She later decided that individual books for each state would be easier for the reader to use. That is why the *Do Your Own Nonprofit* 51-book state series was born. Now in second editions, the *Do Your Own Nonprofit* series has helped thousands of people from all walks of life to start and run successful nonprofits.

BENEVOLANCE

Dr. Bickford started *BenevoLance* (EIN 81-0687426), an international 501(c)(3) that provides intervention for struggling families, elderly and handicapped people, and those in danger due to abuse in the United States, the Philippines, Jamaica, and Serbia, with plans to expand worldwide over time.

BenevoLance fosters global partnerships through networking with other nonprofits, businesses, and other food banks to enrich, support, and enhance the lives of disadvantaged individuals, children, and assist communities through mentoring, raising awareness, and providing tangible assistance to relieve suffering and to increase individual abilities to become self-sustaining. The nonprofit provides needed food and establishes food banks and food distribution centers, shelters, access to medical care, clothing, and education to the needy. They help veterans in need and provide assistive technologies for handicapped individuals. *BenevoLance* helps individuals, families, and communities around the world with sustainable development projects, economic development projects, obtaining clean water and affordable energy, access to improved educational opportunities, job training and internship programs, as well as cultural exchange, disaster relief, and humanitarian aid. *BenevoLance* is the culminating outcome of years of philanthropy, and Kitty wants to touch 10,000+ lives in her lifetime through assistance provided by this nonprofit.

WHAT'S NEXT?

We live in an international culture run by technology. People all over the world have skills and talents to share. Several reputable online venues put buyers of talent together with the talented, but in Kitty's mind, they charge too much for the privilege. She is working on *HumaniTen, Good SamariTens,* and *E-ployment.org* as online marketplaces for buyers and sellers to do business around the world. These services, similar to Fiverr, Freelancer, Upwork, Guru, and others, will charge *reasonable* fees and give 10% of the profit to nonprofits to fund specific project needs. She plans to help her client base initially with funding for their projects, and expand to other organizations over time.

Her goals for *HumaniTen, Good SamariTens,* and *E-ployment.org* include multiple efforts for humans and humanity:

Build: 100 schools in poverty-stricken rural areas of the world, where children cannot afford transportation to get to school and live too far to walk;

Send: 1,000 bright kids to college who would not otherwise be able to go;

Fund: 10,000 nonprofits to make their projects come to life;

Create opportunities for: 100,000 entrepreneurs who have no market for their skills;

Feed: 1,000,000 people, many of them children, who regularly go to bed hungry.

Ambitious goals? YEP! To God be the glory, because she could not do any of those things in her own strength, but she can do all things through Christ who strengthens her (Philippians 4:13).

Pasture Valley's documentary, *"In Faith We Grow"* won best documentary at the Hollywood International Moving Picture Film Festival. See it at www.infaithwegrow.com

THE STORY OF PASTURE VALLEY CHILDREN'S HOME

PART I
INITIAL ORGANIZATIONAL SETUP

CHAPTER 1

PAY ATTENTION:

I AM ONLY GONNA SAY THIS ONCE!

*"If God called us to a task,
He will then qualify us for the job."*
—Jack Hyles

This page is not a sales pitch; it is an offer to relieve you of the logistics of setting up your nonprofit. I stay busy all the time and am not trying to generate new business. Instead, I am offering to make it easier for you if you don't want to become a subject matter specialist on tax-exempt law. Many people have the heart for philanthropic work but get bogged down in the details of the paperwork and quit or never get started. If that describes you, then you may want to hear this!

> MANY PEOPLE HAVE THE HEART FOR PHILANTHROPIC WORK BUT GET BOGGED DOWN IN THE DETAILS OF THE PAPERWORK AND QUIT OR NEVER GET STARTED.

If you would prefer not to have to learn the details of setup and just get to the mission without the paperwork hassle, consider contacting *Tax Exempt 501c3, LLC* to do this work. My fees are *very* reasonable compared to other services, I am normally done in one week or less, guarantee my results (100% IRS acceptance with no rejects ever), am insured for errors and omissions (with no claims ever), and have a track record of over 1,000 happy clients (with no dissatisfied clients).

I will not mention it again in this book, but I wanted you to know that the service is available if you want it.

Dr. Kitty Bickford, DBS, CPC
PO Box 1665, Rolla, MO 65402
(573) 201-4832
kbickford@centurylink.net
www.taxexempt501c3.com

CHAPTER 2

MYTHS ABOUT NONPROFITS

"Twenty years from now you will be more disappointed by the things that you didn't do than by the ones you did do."

—MARK TWAIN

Pasture Valley Children Missions was founded by Dr. Kitty Bickford to provide a hand up, not a handout, to orphans and vulnerable families in Swaziland, Africa.

Starting and running a 501(c)(3) tax-exempt nonprofit is a lot of work, and not everyone is cut out for it. Some go into the venture with false assumptions and myths and later find out they didn't understand what they were getting themselves into. Let's examine some of those myths.

Myth: *Nonprofit* and *tax-exempt* mean the same thing.
Truth: *The state grants nonprofit status. IRS gives tax-exempt status.* Once you get nonprofit status, you can go about your mission and announce to the world that your organization is a legitimate state-approved nonprofit. However, if you do not also go the step further and apply for federal (IRS) *tax-exempt* status, your nonprofit is not eligible for tax deductions for those who make donations (churches and organizations with annual revenues under $5,000 are the exceptions), and the nonprofit does not qualify for most foundation grants.
Moral of this Myth: Apply for federal 501(c)(3) tax-exempt status if you want donations to be tax deductible, and you want to apply for foundation grants.

Myth: I own my nonprofit.
Truth: No, you don't. Nonprofits are not owned. They are run by boards of directors who call the shots and make the decisions. If you are not on the board, you have no control or input into the business of the nonprofit. If you get voted off the board, you are just out. The organization continues without you, even though you may have started it and invested blood, sweat, and tears into building it.
Moral of this Myth: Be very careful who you let on your board of directors.

Myth: I am going to convert my for-profit business to a nonprofit business.

Truth: Conversion is not as simple or easy as it sounds. In most states, you have to dissolve the for-profit business and reapply as a nonprofit. Some states have statutory waiting periods between the two. Also, when you complete the process, you no longer have access to the revenues of the business. The newly formed nonprofit is run by a board of directors who must use the revenue for approved nonprofit purposes only. And remember, you can get voted off your board and if that happens, you lose your business.

Moral of this Myth: Consider keeping your for-profit business (and the profit it makes). Start a nonprofit to handle the philanthropic aspects of your charitable work. *The two must remain separate on paper.* The nonprofit is allowed to benefit from the for-profit, but the for-profit is not allowed to benefit from the nonprofit. If you keep the for-profit business and start a nonprofit, you can donate money to the nonprofit (and take the tax deduction) and share assets (equipment, furniture, building space, etc.) with the nonprofit, but maintain unregulated use of the for-profit revenues without board or IRS oversight. You cannot have the same name for the nonprofit as you have for the for-profit business, but you can have a similar name, or come up with a different name. For example, suppose you had a thriving for-profit educational tutoring business called *Education Ventures*. You could name your nonprofit that tutors kids for free *Education Adventures*.

Myth: I am going to set up my nonprofit as a limited liability corporation (LLC).

Truth: A few states allow nonprofits to register as LLCs. However, IRS does not allow it for 501(c)(3) tax-exempt status. Why? Because an LLC is a for-profit entity, and a nonprofit is a not-for-profit entity. The two do not mix. The only exception is if every member of the LLC is a nonprofit organization.

Moral of this Myth: Choose *corporation* as the nonprofit entity. Fewer headaches, more protection for board members against personal liability, and no IRS rejections for filing the wrong entity.

Myth: I am starting a foundation to give out school supplies to kids who cannot afford them. I can't wait to see their little faces when I give them new backpacks and markers!

Truth: Foundations cannot provide direct aid to individuals, but public charities can. Although foundations and public charities are both classified as types of 501(c)(3) nonprofits, they are not the same. Many foundations are set up by corporations or wealthy philanthropists who want to give money to worthwhile causes instead of giving it to IRS for income tax. Because foundations can (and often are) run by families or specific corporations, they are more highly regulated and operate under different rules than public charities. For example, donations to foundations are only deductible up to 30% of adjusted gross income. For public charities, it is 50% of adjusted gross income.

Foundations must give away a percentage of revenues every year (with some exceptions) while public charities have no such requirements. Foundations can only give funding to other 501(c) approved organizations and must prove due diligence to IRS for every grant they give. Foundations demonstrate due diligence by getting copies of the organization's IRS approval documentation to prove the organization is tax-exempt, and a copy of the most recent nonprofit tax return to show that the organization is in good standing with IRS. Organizations that have not filed their first nonprofit tax return with IRS typically do not get approved for grants. Foundations don't want to get into trouble with IRS for not being diligent.

School kids needing backpacks do not have IRS credentials or nonprofit tax returns, and foundations cannot give out school supplies directly to children. They work through public charities or other nonprofits by giving them grants to buy school supplies and hope that is what the organizations actually do with the money. Public charities must exercise prudence but are allowed to work directly with people when performing their missions so that public charities can give out backpacks and markers directly to kids. If you want to work directly with people, start a public charity, not a foundation.

Many organizations choose to use the word *foundation* in their names when they are actually public charities. Although IRS allows it, confusion sometimes happens. For example, when a public charity applies to a foundation for a grant but has the word *foundation* in the organization's name, the foundation giving the grant may wonder why another foundation is applying to them for money. Foundations generally give money, not ask for grants. When there is only so much money available for grants, foundations have to find a ways to weed out applicants so that they can pick the most worthwhile causes to fund. Don't give them a reason to weed out your organization by calling yourself a foundation when you are not. Think of it this way: Would you call yourself an apple if you were hanging on an orange tree? Both are fruits, but that is where the similarity ends. It is the same with public charities and foundations. Both are 501(c)(3) tax-exempt nonprofits, but that is where the similarity ends.

Moral of this Myth: Choose your status carefully. Public Charity status is the gold standard of 501(c)(3) tax-exempt nonprofits. Foundations work well if you plan to have all family on your board and you plan to do your own funding or fund through a corporation you own or control.

Myth: I am going to be president of my nonprofit and make $100,000 a year!

Truth: It is not *your* nonprofit, and most nonprofit boards are manned by volunteers (especially small nonprofits just starting out) who receive no compensation except for reimbursement of reasonable costs associated with fulfilling their roles as board members. When you get big enough to have salaries, the board votes on the jobs that need to be filled, the hours, the pay, and the job descriptions. The board hires people who work *for* the board and report *to* the board. If the board hires you as a program director or some other function you are most qualified for, you are not being paid in your capacity as a board member, and you cannot vote on your pay. When the board vote starts, you should leave the room to avoid a conflict of interest. If you are on the board and going to be an employee, you have no input into your salary as a hired employee of the organization.

Moral of this Myth: Roll up your sleeves and get ready to do a lot of hard work to grow your organization to the point that you can draw a salary as a program director or employee of the board. Don't expect to get rich being the president of a fledgling nonprofit.

Myth: I will put all family members on the board of directors, and we will control the organization.

Truth: You can put just family members on the board, but IRS will look at the composition of family members. If more than 49% of the board is made up of related people, there is a chance that IRS will flag your tax-exempt application for follow-up by an IRS agent, and your request for approval as a public charity may be reclassified as a foundation. Is 49% written anywhere? No, but call IRS at 877-829-5500 and ask what percentage of a nonprofit board for a public charity can be family. The answer will be something like, "Although we do not specify in statutes, we want to see less than half the board made up of related members." Additional queries will reveal that IRS frowns on public charities that are controlled by related people. Public charities exist for the benefit of the public, not for the benefit of family members. Knowing that IRS has the power to approve or delay your application, don't give them this reason to hold up your approval. You can always add members later and report those changes to IRS in your annual report.

Moral of this Myth: To avoid any complications in processing your application, make sure that at least 51% of your board of directors are unrelated.

Myth: I didn't apply to IRS for 501(c) (3) tax-exempt status, so I don't have to file federal annual nonprofit tax returns.

Truth: All nonprofits (except churches) must file annual tax returns with IRS. Over 650,000 nonprofits have made the mistake of not filing required tax returns and have had their present (or future!) tax-exempt status revoked. When the deadline to file for the third consecutive year comes and goes, IRS computers make a note that an organization is automatically revoked from 501(c) (3) status, even if that organization has never applied. If the nonprofit later applies, IRS will review the application, approve it, and put the info in the IRS computer, which will spit out an approval letter. The organization will get it a week later in the mail, and the board will be jubilant because they got approved for 501(c) (3) status. Officers will tell all their friends, post it on Facebook, send out a tweet, and announce a big fundraiser. When they open the mail the next day, they receive a letter from IRS saying that their 501(c) (3) was automatically revoked for failure to file taxes for three consecutive years. To get the status back, the nonprofit must reapply and give IRS good reasons to reinstate the organization. They must justify why they didn't file each year individually (with proof) and all years cumulatively, and pay the filing fee again. Exceptions are churches, they do not have to file tax returns. Other organizations must file a return regardless of revenues. However, the appropriate schedules must be attached to the federal application for 501(c) (3) to avoid being revoked for organizations that fall into the *under $5,000* category.

Moral of this Myth: If you have not filed your nonprofit taxes, do not apply for federal 501(c) (3) status until you catch up (and are sure IRS has the returns recorded in their computer system). If many years have gone by and you have had over $5,000 annual revenue, you might just start a new nonprofit from scratch and let the other nonprofit die a quiet death in a lonely corner of the closet where the paperwork is stored. It is sometimes easier and wiser to start over rather than go through the hassles of resurrecting a dead paper trail of a nonprofit that has delinquent filings with the state or IRS. Once you get reinstated by the feds, then many states want missing filings as well. It can turn into an expensive and time-consuming process to get caught up for the years you missed. Because nonprofit records are public records, it might be easier to pick a new name and start over so that your organization has a clean paper trail.

Myth: Nonprofits are not allowed to make a profit from their activities.
Truth: Of course they can! How can a business stay in business if it does not make a profit? According to the *Council of Nonprofits*, less than 10% of revenues come from individual donations to nonprofits. The breakdown looks something like this: 30% of revenues from government sources, 50% from fees for services provided by the nonprofit, and the rest from foundation grants, investments, corporate donations, and other sources. Yes, nonprofits can and should make a profit. If they do not generate revenue above expenses, how can they continue to exist or expand in the future?

Nonprofit organizations can make a profit; they just cannot spend it to benefit individuals unless those individuals are part of their target mission. A nonprofit can buy a new pair of shoes for an orphan, but not a new pair of shoes for the board president.
Moral of this Myth: Plan for and expect to have excess revenue over expenses. The alternative is not self-sustaining.

Myth: If we are running our nonprofit efficiently, our indirect and administrative overhead should be small.

Truth: Not necessarily. If you are running a tutoring program for at-risk kids, you might get volunteers willing to do the work, but if you are running a mental health facility for war veterans with Post Traumatic Stress Disorder (PTSD), you need trained therapists and credentialed counselors. If you are running a nonprofit charter school, teachers need to buy groceries and pay mortgages just as public school teachers do. Skilled professionals cannot afford to work for free; you have to pay them reasonable wages for the skills they provide to your nonprofit. It is possible that your highest expense could be salaries. That doesn't mean you are doing anything wrong. As long as the wages paid are comparable to other nonprofits of similar size and mission, and as long as the work is getting done, write the check!

Moral of this Myth: Spend what is prudent to provide the best services you can to fulfill your mission. Get the best people you can afford and treat them well so they will want to stay and grow with the organization.

Myth: Grants are easy to get if you have 501(c)(3) status.

Truth: Just because you apply for a grant does not mean you are going to get it. New nonprofits with no track record of success are not likely to get grant money. Many think they can hire a hotshot grant writer who will bring in big bucks. The truth is that there are only so many grant dollars available, and grantmakers choose the organizations with proven success that have the most potential to have the biggest impact. New nonprofits often have not reached a competitive level yet. Board members often blame grant writers because they didn't get the grants, but in reality, they should have channeled their efforts into creating a group of supporters to make repeated contributions instead of chasing elusive grant money.

To write a big grant (meaning $100K - $1,000,000+), the grant writer will spend weeks to months preparing the grant package. Grants are highly competitive and even leaving out one tiny detail in a grant package can cause the grant to be denied. Grant writers often charge a flat fee to start ($5K – 25K), and then a percentage of the grant, often 10%. That creates a problem for many organizations because most grants have a stipulation that you cannot pay grant writers from the proceeds of the grant. That means that the organization must pay the grant writer out of general operating funds. If those funds are not available, the organization cannot hire the grant writer. If the organization does not get the grant, they have already spent the flat fee, which somewhat compensated the grant writer for preparing the submission.

Moral of this Myth: Establish a proven track record of success before applying for grants. Select grant writers carefully. You get what you pay for. Pick grant writers with multiple proven successes, and expect to pay good money for their talents and skills. Verify their prior grants with the organizations that were approved. Check with the organization and also with the grantmaker. Pick up the phone or take the time to write to the organizations involved. If the grant writer will not give you organization and foundation names and amounts, move on. Many grant writers will say they are protecting the privacy of the organizations they worked with. Not true! Everything about grants is public record and can be verified on both the nonprofit recipient's tax return and the grantmaker's tax return. They are both public record. The truth might be that the grant writer has no success and doesn't want to tell you. Good grant writers are worth their hire and can mean the difference in an organization growing or maintaining the status quo. Don't blame the grant writer if you do not get funded. Many variables go into the selection process, and lots of the considerations have nothing to do with the grant writer.

Myth: We can expand our mission later when we have more resources.
Truth: IRS and the state approve you for a particular mission. If you choose to expand it, you have to report the change to IRS when you file your annual tax return. At that point, IRS can approve or deny your request. I ran into that problem with *Pasture Valley*

Children Missions. It was set up to work with orphans, orphanages, and vulnerable families in Swaziland, Africa. Unfortunately, we were only able to find four grants that dealt with both orphans and Swaziland. That was not an enormous pool of potential funding when compared to the size of the HIV/AIDS orphan problem in that country. After a few years, we wanted to expand the mission to other countries and to include other philanthropic pursuits (shelters for abused women, economic development projects, water treatment and access, etc.). Our mission did not cover those things, and we had no authority to pursue philanthropy in the United States. To fix the situation, I started a second nonprofit, *BenevoLance*. I made the mission extremely broad for this second nonprofit so that we had room to grow without having to start a third nonprofit.

Moral of this Myth: Write your mission wider than your current narrow focus regarding geographic location and activities so that five years down the road, you don't have to go back to IRS and start over or deal with red tape to get approval to expand. Write a broad mission now as you get started, so you have the option to grow in different directions later. Just because you are approved for a certain mission does not mean you have to be working on that specific mission at any given time. You can work on what your board decides is the best focus for the organization at the current time. Additional things you are approved for can wait for the future. You are not obligated to pursue every aspect of your mission simultaneously. Think big and apply big the first time!

Myth: I need a huge board of directors (or I don't need a board at all, just me).

Truth: About half the states require one board member minimum, the other half require at least three. Only New Hampshire requires five. However, just about every state specifies in their statutes which positions need to be filled and what combinations are not allowed. For example, many states prohibit the board president from also being the secretary or treasurer. Even if the state does not specify, IRS scrutinizes any board of less than three unrelated board members. If you call them (and I have several times to see if I got the same answer every time) at 877-829-5500 and ask what the minimum number of board members is, you will get this answer: "IRS statutes do not specify a minimum number of board members."

Next, ask, "How many board members does IRS want to see so that the number of board members is not an issue?"

The answer: "Three unrelated board members or five if two are related."

Moral of this Myth: Pick at least three unrelated board members and be done with it, or five members if two are related. Board members do not have to be in the same state, and if your mission is international, they don't even have to be in the same country. Note: Cousins, aunts, and uncles are not on the IRS list of relatives, but ancestors are. Go figure...

Myth: I can use the money for my nonprofit for anything I want.

Truth: No, you cannot. The Board of Directors approves all expenditures, and each expense must relate to the nonprofit mission. You cannot use the money to pay your electric bill or car insurance just because you generated the income. All nonprofit revenues belong to the nonprofit and must be used for the approved nonprofit mission.

Moral of this Myth: Make sure you have other income to sustain your needs before deciding to pursue your nonprofit mission full time. If you are a salaried employee of the nonprofit and are performing needed functions on behalf of the nonprofit, the board can pay you reasonable compensation for services actually rendered. You are not getting paid to be on the board; you are getting paid in a second capacity as an employee of the board.

Myth: If I give a building, vehicle, computer, book I wrote, or whatever to the nonprofit and later close the nonprofit, I can just change the copyright, deed, or title back into my name again, or take the property back.

Truth: When an asset of any kind becomes the legal property of a nonprofit, it can never go back to the person who donated it. If the nonprofit closes, the asset must be given to another nonprofit, or the court can decide the disposition of the asset. In no case can it go to an individual.

Moral of this Myth: If you want to retain a claim on physical property, loan it to the nonprofit, do not deed it or gift it. Once it is gone, it is gone forever, and you have no claim to it. If instead you choose to loan it, the organization gets the benefit, but you still own it. That includes books. Keep your book copyright in your own name, and donate royalties if and when you want to, but don't give your book to the nonprofit. You cannot get the rights back later.

Myth: We are going to start a hybrid social enterprise organization and get 501(c)(3) status.

Truth: Hybrid organizations are part for-profit, part nonprofit. Some states have approved them, but IRS is not likely to approve this type of organization. For one thing, it is too new and laws have not caught up. For another, for-profit organizations are not eligible for 501(c)(3) tax-exempt status.

Moral of this Myth: Don't waste your time and money. Follow the path that gets you approved!

CHAPTER 3

IS 501(C) (3) STATUS RIGHT FOR YOU?

I can do all things through Christ who strengthens me.
—Philippians 4:13 NKJV

STEP-BY-STEP INSTRUCTIONS

So, you have this great idea for a nonprofit floating around in your head, but just don't know what to do with it. If so, you are not alone. Many people want to make a difference in the world, but they either don't know how, can't afford an attorney to set it up, or they get buried in the mountain of paperwork needed to get 501(c) (3) tax-exempt status.

I want to make the setup easy for you. I know from personal experience the areas that are the most difficult (so much so that many people give up because it is just too hard). This book gives you step-by-step instructions on what to do in the correct order for your state, how to do it, where to do it, how long it takes, who to call, and what it costs. Just that information saves much time and aggravation. But that is not all you get.

> THIS BOOK GIVES YOU STEP-BY-STEP INSTRUCTIONS ON WHAT TO DO IN THE CORRECT ORDER FOR YOUR STATE, HOW TO DO IT,

ASK ME 3 SPECIFIC QUESTIONS

You get to ask me three specific questions during your 501(c)(3) project. It is my way of saying thank you for buying my book. Just go to *www.doyourownnonprofit.com* or *www.taxexempt501c3.com* and contact me. I am glad to help you! But that is not all. I have gone the extra mile and given you great resources I wish I would have had that will remove the most frustrating part of the tax-exempt process: paperwork!

FILL IN THE BLANK STATE TEMPLATES

Does the thought of preparing articles of organization, bylaws, conflict of interest policies, and board meeting minutes make you nervous? Your stomach queasy? Fill you with dread? Make you want to forget the whole idea?

I had the same feelings when I started Pasture Valley Children Missions, so I hired a $300-an-hour attorney on your behalf to develop fill-in-the-blank templates of the documents that were cumbersome and time-consuming. All you have to do is pay a small fee to download the right forms (fee goes to support my nonprofits), fill in the blanks, print, and mail. Now you can do the state and in-house paperwork in 30 minutes with full assurance of the legal integrity of the documents.

EXAMPLES OF APPROVED NONPROFITS

A picture is worth a thousand words, so I researched other 501(c)(3) organizations, and in Appendix A, you will find links to their paperwork. These links are also live on *www.doyourownnonprofit.com* website. Find an organization like the one you are starting and study their federal application before filling out yours.

I hope that the benefits of the book, website, templates, and access to paperwork from other nonprofits make your experience easy, and I hope you will contact me if you run into trouble so we can figure it out together. Now let's look at the benefits of starting a tax-exempt organization.

BENEFITS OF 501(C) (3) TAX- EXEMPT STATUS

People pursue 501(c) (3) status for different reasons. In addition to the intangible rewards (satisfaction, doing the right thing, helping people, feeling good about your efforts), there are tangible reasons to pursue your mission as a tax-exempt organization.

Below are a few of the more tangible benefits:

- Tax deductions to contributors
- Limited liability
- Perpetual existence and permanence
- Eligibility for grants
- Tax-exempt purchasing power in some states
- Reduced postage
- Discounted internet service provider costs
- Public service announcements on the radio and other media at little or no charge

Getting to the approval process with the Internal Revenue Service (IRS) requires that you complete many steps along the way. This state guide is designed to get you there quickly with no unnecessary steps, wasted effort, or scratching your head wondering what to do next. The best part is that you do not have to hire an attorney to do the paperwork for you. If you can follow a checklist and simple instructions, you can complete the requirements to get tax-exempt status.

IRS states that for an organization to be tax-exempt, it must be "organized and operated exclusively for exempt purposes set forth in Section 501(c) (3)..."

Those exempt purposes include:

- Charitable
- Religious
- Educational
- Scientific
- Literary

- Testing for public safety (although contributions are not tax deductible)
- Fostering national or international sports competition
- Preventing cruelty to children and animals

IRS DIRECTIVE

Here's how the IRS looks at the status:

... the term charitable is used in its generally accepted legal sense and includes relief of the poor, the distressed, or the underprivileged; advancement of religion; advancement of education or science; erecting or maintaining public buildings, monuments, or works; lessening the burdens of government; lessening neighborhood tensions; eliminating prejudice and discrimination; defending human and civil rights secured by law; and combating community deterioration and juvenile delinquency.

CHURCHES AND RELIGIOUS ENTITIES

Religious nonprofits are harder to pinpoint but form a class of exemption with some commonalities. If it looks like a church, acts like a church, operates like a church, and feels like a church, then it is probably a church. However, a church must have:

- distinct religious beliefs and denomination
- a location to meet
- a schedule of services on a regular basis
- a stable group of people that make up the congregation

Proof of the above aspects may be required to get the exemption. IRS defines *church* to also include synagogues, temples, and mosques.

In the list below are those organizations that do not have to file the 501(c) (3) application as they are automatically exempt:

- Churches
- Interchurch organizations of the local units of the church
- Conventions or associations of churches
- Integrated auxiliaries of a church (such as a men's or women's organization)
- Religious school
- Mission society
- Youth group

Churches are automatically exempt without filing 501(c) (3) paperwork with IRS. They just have to make sure they mark the church box when they get their federal employer identification number. Many churches still choose to file for 501(c) (3) tax-exempt status because it assures their tithers and donors that contributions qualify for tax deductions. Church auxiliary organizations can fall under the church umbrella for 501(c) (3) purposes under certain circumstances. The benefit of being under that umbrella is that there is no requirement to file an annual return with IRS.

Many other religious organizations that are not churches under IRS codes may still qualify for tax-exempt status as religious organizations, but unlike churches, they have to file annual information tax returns. These might include:

- Mission organizations
- Speakers' organizations
- Nondenominational ministries
- Ecumenical organizations
- Faith-based social agencies
- Evangelistic ministries

EDUCATIONAL ORGANIZATIONS

The IRS definition of educational organizations includes schools at all levels from elementary to college and beyond, as well as trade schools, correspondence schools, and schools that provide education through media such as internet, television, and radio. Some other types of organizations that may not be immediately obvious as educational may qualify for tax-exemption as educational organizations:

- Museums
- Zoos
- Planetariums
- Symphony orchestras
- Organizations that conduct public discussion groups, forums, panels, and lectures

In addition, nonprofit daycare centers and youth sports organizations may qualify as educational tax-exempt organizations.

SCIENTIFIC ORGANIZATIONS

Scientific organizations that want 501(c)(3) status must demonstrate that their research is in the public interest. That is done by using the results (including patents, copyrights, processes, or formulas) in nondiscriminatory ways for the public good. The research can be for science, education, publications available to the public, curing disease, or helping attract new industry to an area. Research does not include product testing.

LITERARY ORGANIZATIONS

Literary organizations seeking 501(c)(3) status must be able to show that any sales or publishing they do is related to their tax-exempt purpose.

AMATEUR ATHLETIC ORGANIZATIONS

Amateur athletic organizations fall into two categories:

1. Those that promote national or international amateur sports competition but do not supply facilities or equipment, and
2. Those that exclusively develop athletes and/or conduct national or international amateur sports competition and provide facilities and equipment, even though the membership is local or regional.

> **NOTE:** Little league, soccer camps, and other youth sports organizations qualify for 501(c)(3) status as youth organizations and do not have to be involved in national or international sports competitions.

ORGANIZATIONS THAT PREVENT CRUELTY TO CHILDREN AND ANIMALS

Organizations that seek to prevent cruelty to children and animals may:

- Try to protect children forced into dangerous jobs
- Advocate alternatives to child abuse
- Seek humane treatment for laboratory animals
- Assist in animal population control
- Provide shelters for abused animals
- Make other attempts to reduce cruelty to animals or children

SEPARATE ENTITY FROM FOUNDERS

Your organization must be set up and organized in such a way that IRS recognizes it as a separate entity from its founders. In other words, the people who start it do not own it. It is not their organization; it is separate and perpetual and will survive even if the founders do not. For this reason, be careful not to call yourself the owner of a 501(c) (3) organization (especially when dealing with IRS). You can start the organization. You can be on the board. You can president of the board. You can be an advisor to the board. However, you cannot be an owner. A tax-exempt organization is *NOT* owned. One individual does not operate it; it is normally governed and run by a board of directors, and there are distinct rules about the number and relationships of those on the board (covered in a later chapter).

NOT FOR PRIVATE INTEREST

Section 501(c) (3) status *DOES NOT* apply to organizations created for the benefit of private interests or those that do not receive a substantial part of their income from the general public or the government. You cannot get 501(c) (3) status so that you or your family or friends can benefit from the tax-exempt status. It must benefit the public to be eligible for 501(c) (3). Your organization also cannot be set up to benefit a specific person or organization. You cannot participate in political campaigns directly or indirectly at any level, but you can have educational meetings, create educational materials, and appear before government bodies. You may not participate in illegal activities.

The following types of organizations **DO NOT** qualify for 501(c) (3) status:

- 501(c) (1) organizations: Instrumentalities of the United States organized under an act of Congress (such as Federal Credit Unions).
- 501(c) (2) organizations: Title holding corporations for exempt organizations that collect and pay income from property to exempt organizations.
- 501(c) (4) organizations: Civic leagues, social welfare organizations, local associations of employees.
- 501(c) (5) organizations: Labor, agriculture, and horticultural organizations.

501(c) (6) organizations: Business leagues, chambers of commerce, and real estate boards.

501(c) (7) organizations: Social and recreational clubs.

501(c) (8) organizations: Fraternal beneficiary societies and associations.

501(c) (9) organizations: Voluntary employee beneficiary associations.

501(c) (10) organizations: Domestic fraternal societies, orders, or associations.

501(c) (11) organizations: Teacher's Retirement Funds.

501(c) (12) organizations: Local benevolent life insurance associations, mutual ditch or irrigation companies, mutual or cooperative electric or telephone companies and like organizations.

501(c) (13) organizations: Cemetery companies.

501(c) (14) organizations: State chartered credit unions.

501(c) (15) organizations: Small insurance companies and associations providing insurance to members substantially at cost.

501(c) (16) organizations: Cooperative organizations to finance crop operations.

501(c) (17) organizations: Supplemental unemployment benefit trusts.

501(c) (18) organizations: Employee-funded pension trusts created before 1959.

501(c) (19) organizations: War veterans' organizations.

501(c) (20) organizations: Group legal services plan organizations.

501(c) (21) organizations: Black lung benefit trusts.

501(c) (22) organizations: Withdrawal liability payment funds.

501(c) (23) organizations: Veterans' organizations created before 1880.

501(c) (25) organizations: Title holding corporations or trusts with multiple parents.

501(c) (26) organizations: State-sponsored organizations providing health coverage for high-risk individuals.

501(c) (27) organizations: State-sponsored Worker's Compensation reinsurance organizations.

501(c) (28) organizations: National Railroad Retirement Investment Trusts.

501(d) organizations: Religious and apostolic organizations (communal religious communities).

501(e) organizations: Cooperative hospital service organizations.

501(f) organizations: Cooperative service organizations of operating educational organizations that perform collective investment services for educational organizations.

501(k) organizations: Child care organizations.

501(n) organizations: Charitable risk pools that pool certain insurance risks of 501(c) (3) organizations.

521(a) organizations: Farmers' cooperative organizations.

527 organizations: Political organizations accepting contributions or making expenditures for political campaigns.

Now that you know the basic nonprofit categories, let's get you organized with a checklist so you can track your progress as you make it.

CHAPTER 4

DO-IT-YOURSELF CHECKLIST

"Every great dream begins with a dreamer. Always remember, you have within you the strength, the patience, and the passion to reach for the stars to change the world."

—HARRIET TUBMAN

Francis of Assisi said that you eat an elephant one bite at a time, so before you become overwhelmed with the process, just concentrate on taking the bite in front of you, and when you swallow that requirement, go on to the next bite. You will be surprised how quickly you can devour the whole proverbial elephant and form a nonprofit corporation that is state and federally recognized. Each chapter of this book is written in a specific order to help you do the required steps in the right order the first time.

> YOU WILL BE SURPRISED HOW QUICKLY YOU CAN DEVOUR THE WHOLE PROVERBIAL ELEPHANT AND FORM A NONPROFIT CORPORATION THAT IS STATE AND FEDERALLY RECOGNIZED.

INITIAL SETUP

___Determine the tax-exempt purpose (you can choose more than one)
    ___charitable
    ___religious
    ___educational
    ___scientific
    ___literary
    ___testing for public safety
    ___fostering sports competition
    ___preventing cruelty to children
    ___preventing cruelty to animals
___Select business name and make sure it is available
___Is Inc. or Corp. required in business name?
    ___Yes
    ___No
___Get a Federal Employer Identification Number (FEIN)
___Develop a strong mission statement
___Form a board of directors
___*Prepare and file Articles of Incorporation
___*Prepare Bylaws
___*Develop Conflict of Interest Policy and Annual Statements
___*Hold and document the first board meeting

*If you don't want to develop your own Articles of Incorporation, bylaws, conflict of interest documents, and initial organizational meeting minutes from scratch, go to *www.doyourownnonprofit.com* and download the documents and templates to make it fast. The fee for these documents helps fund transportation costs for kids to go to school in Mhlosheni, Swaziland as part of Pasture Valley Children Missions.*

DO YOU QUALIFY FOR FORM 1023-EZ INSTEAD OF FORM 1023?

___Do You Qualify for the Form 1023-EZ Streamlined Filing? If you answer yes to the next three items, you qualify for the streamlined filing instead of the long filing. You get to skip Chapters 14 – 33 and go straight to Chapter 34.
    ___Our mission is strictly in the USA with no international involvement or board members.
    ___Our projected budget is under $50,000 a year for the first three years.
    ___We are not starting a church, school, hospital, or research facility.

COMPLETE IRS FORM 1023 (APPLICATION FOR TAX-EXEMPT STATUS) IF YOU DO NOT QUALIFY FOR FORM 1023-EZ

___Part I, Identification of Applicant
___Part II, Organizational Structure
___Part III, Provisions in your Documents
___Part IV, Narrative Description of Your Activities
___Part V, Compensation and Other Financial Arrangements
___Part VI, Your Members and Other Individuals and Organizations the Receive Benefits from You
___Part VII, Your History
___Part VIII, Specific Activities
___Part IX, Financial Data
___Part X, Public Charity Status
___Part XI, User Fee Information
___Required Schedules (A – H)
    ___ Schedule A: Churches
    ___ Schedule B: Schools, Colleges, and Universities
    ___ Schedule C: Hospitals and Medical Research Organizations

___ Schedule D: Section 509(a) (3) Supporting Organization
___ Schedule E: Organizations Not Filing Form 1023 Within 27 Months of Formation
___ Schedule F: Homes for the Elderly or Handicapped and Low-Income Housing
___ Schedule G: Successors to Other Organizations
___ Schedule H: Scholarships, Fellowships, Educational Loans, Or Other Grants

FOLLOW UP TASKS

___ Annual Information Tax Return Required by IRS
___ Submit PS Form 3624, *Application to Mail at Nonprofit Standard Mail Rates*

CHAPTER 5

SELECT A BUSINESS NAME AND MAKE SURE IT IS AVAILABLE

"The difference between the impossible and the possible lies in a man's determination."

—Tommy Lasorda

DESIGNATE ORGANIZATION TYPE AND SUFFIX

Most nonprofits are corporations because founders have the most personal protection from lawsuits and other legal matters, and the nonprofit is eligible for more grants than other forms of organization. Some states do not allow you to register other organization types, so corporation is your only choice.

Don't let the designation *corporation* scare you. You can start small and stay small, or start small and grow huge. That depends on what you do to grow the organization. Some states require a designation suffix at the end of the organization name such as *Inc., Corp, Incorporated,* or *Corporation*. I set up Pasture Valley Children Missions in Missouri where no suffix is required, but it is optional. Michigan forbids using a suffix. Florida requires a suffix (even for churches!), so the name would have been Pasture Valley Children Missions, Inc. It just depends on where you live.

> **In Minnesota, a suffix is NOT required.**

PICK A GREAT NAME

You must have a unique name, different from all other business and organization names in the state. Also, be careful not to pick something too close to well-known nonprofits, even if they are in another state. Very similar names can cause confusion as well as claims of infringement from the other nonprofit. Spend some time thinking about what your organization represents and come up with a name that fits what you plan to do.

When you select a name for your nonprofit, keep it short and explanatory. Leave off words like *charity, organization, nonprofit,* and *foundation* (unless you are a foundation, which is different from a public charity). You might also want to leave off *The* at the beginning of the organization's name. IRS does not put *The* in their records, but states do. It could confuse donors who try to check you out when the two names do not match between the state and IRS, and they cannot find you in the IRS database. Best to leave *The* out of the name. In any case, you want the name to fit the mission, be easy to remember, and have hearing appeal.

Let me give you some examples of what I mean:

- If you had vision problems, which would you contact first? *Visual Impairment League* or *Modern Vision Clinic*? Most people would contact *Modern Vision Clinic* because it sounds state-of-the-art and is easy to understand.

- If you wanted to get a pet for your kids but didn't want to spend a lot of money, would you select *Storm Cat Rescue* (an actual nonprofit in North Carolina) or *Animal Welfare League of Montgomery County* (an actual nonprofit in Maryland)?
- If you were selecting a Christian daycare center for your toddler, would you pick *The Institute of Divine Developmental and Cognitive Child Care* or *All God's Kids*? Most people would pick *All God's Kids* because it is friendly, short, easy to remember, and makes a statement about how the organization feels about children.
- If you were looking for some help with a legal matter but had limited funds, would you contact *Criminal and Civil Litigation Foundation* or *Legal Aid Services*? If you are like me, you pick the one that isn't a mouthful of gobbledygook.

For my first organization, I chose *Pasture Valley Children Missions*. We get donation checks in that say *Pasture Valley Children's Mission*. If I had been smart back then, I would have just called it *Pasture Valley Children* because it fits on a check more easily and isn't confusing. I learned my lesson and named the second nonprofit *BenevoLance* (The website for benevolence was already taken, and *Lance* lent itself to an attractive logo that projected taking the Sword of the Lord [the power of Jehovah] to poor of the world).

People like to keep it simple. My friend Judy Hanna wrote a book called *Ageism Activism*. It was a wonderful book of resources and information about how to spot elderly and senior abuse and discrimination and what to do about it. The book didn't do well until she changed the name to *Should I Be Afraid?* Then she got lots of readers' attention. The same holds true with your nonprofit. Get lots of attention by picking a clever, catchy, short, and explanatory name. Pick a name that rolls smoothly off the tongue and lends itself to an attractive or memorable logo. Leave off words that add nothing to the meaning, and keep it short so it fits on a donation check. When in doubt, explain your nonprofit to 8-year-olds and ask them what you should call it. They will know!

IS THE NAME AVAILABLE?

Next, check with the state's corporation division to find out if the name is available. You can call the state's corporation division, or you can check name availability online by Googling the state combined with "business entity search."

Now that you have decided what to call your nonprofit, your next step will be to get a Federal Employer Identification Number. Details follow in the next chapter.

CHAPTER 6

GET A FEDERAL EMPLOYER IDENTIFICATION NUMBER (FEIN)

"What you finish is more important than what you begin."
—Mike Murdock

FEDERAL EMPLOYER IDENTIFICATION NUMBER (FEIN)

The Federal Employer Identification Number (FEIN) is like a social security number for all kinds of businesses, whether for-profit or nonprofit. It is a nine-digit number assigned for tax filing and reporting purposes. The FEIN format is XX – XXXXXXX, different from social security numbers in which the format is XXX – XX – XXXX.

As confusing as it may seem – with the word *employer* in its name – you do not have to employ anyone to need this number. And to be even more confusing, it goes by other names. It is sometimes referred to as:

- Employer Identification Number (EIN),
- Tax Identification Number or Tax ID Number (TIN), and
- IRS Form CP 575 E (If you register it correctly, the letter E will be on the end for exempt organizations on the CP 575 confirmation notice)
- SS-4. This is the mail-in or fax-in application to get an EIN. IRS returns the number handwritten on the SS-4, so some people confuse the application with the number and call the FEIN the SS-4.

The FEIN does not designate your organization as tax-exempt. Rather it identifies the organization as an *existing recognized business entity*. You must have the FEIN to open a bank account for your nonprofit organization, and some states require that number to file your incorporation with the state. Make sure the organization name is the same with IRS as it is with the state, including any suffix (such as Inc. or Corp.) that you included in the name.

Only one FEIN is assigned to an organization, and it never expires, even if not used for a long time. You cannot get a new FEIN for the same organization if you lose the number or forget it. If you lose the number and you have set up a bank account, you can contact the bank, and they can look it up. You can contact IRS by calling the Business and Specialty Tax Line at (800) 829-4933. They will give you the Tax ID number over the phone if you are an authorized person (such as an officer of the organization).

You cannot use an EIN from another business you already have. A nonprofit is a separate entity, and you must register it with IRS separately. You can have a dozen EINs for different businesses, but you still need a new one for the nonprofit.

THE FEIN DOES NOT DESIGNATE YOUR ORGANIZATION AS TAX-EXEMPT.

FEIN is free. IRS does not charge a fee to get this number, but lots of websites want to charge $49 to $79 to get it for you. You can do this yourself in five minutes at no charge.

The word *The* at the beginning of an organization's name will not show up in the EIN paperwork or IRS database. Also, the only punctuation and special characters allowed on the EIN application are hyphen (-) and ampersand (&). That means you leave off all commas, periods, etc. For example, IRS would process *The John Smith Evangelical Ministries, Inc.* as *JOHN SMITH EVANGELICAL MINISTRIES INC*

TWO WAYS TO GET AN FEIN NUMBER:

1. THE ONLINE OPTION

The easiest and fastest way to get an EIN is online between 7 a.m. and 10 p.m. Eastern time Monday through Friday. You get the FEIN in real time. The online option is not available nights, weekends, or holidays. Do an internet search for "FEIN ONLINE" and click on the IRS link. There will be other links that want to charge you; skip them and click on the IRS link. Here is the link you want: *https://www.irs.gov/businesses/small-businesses-self-employed/apply-for-an-employer-identification-number-ein-online* which leads you to this link (you can go directly if you type it in): *https://sa.www4.irs.gov/modiein/individual/index.jsp*

> **NOTE:** You need a social security number to get an Employer Identification Number issued online. If no one on your board has a social, you can use an Individual Taxpayer Identification Number (ITIN) and mail or fax in the request using Form SS-4. For foreign organizations, write *FOREIGN* where it asks for your social security number. If no one on the board has a social or ITIN, someone on the board may want to apply for an ITIN using IRS Form W-7, or you can ask a U. S. citizen to join your board. ITINs take about seven weeks to come back.

Some notes on what to click on using the online FEIN application:

1. Your Type of Legal Structure answer is: *View additional types including Tax-Exempt and Government Organizations.*
2. Additional Types: If you are setting up a church, click on *church*. Otherwise, click on *Other Nonprofit/Tax Exempt Organizations* at the bottom of the screen.
3. Why is the Nonprofit Requesting an EIN? Answer: *Started a new business*
4. Who is the Responsible Party? Answer: *Individual*
5. You will need to put your name and social security number as they appear on your social security card. Anyone on your board of directors can put in their name and social. That is how IRS ensures that a person from the U.S. is applying and not some international terrorist group or something trying to funnel money through a nonprofit into illegal activities. Using your social to get a nonprofit EIN does *not* affect your personal income tax return in any way. IRS just needs a warm body with a social to get the EIN online. Once you enter the name and social, click on *I am a responsible and duly authorized member or officer having knowledge of the organization's affairs.* If the responsible party changes over time, you have to notify IRS of the new responsible party on Form 8822-B.
6. When you put in the physical address for the nonprofit (which can be your address at home; you don't need to get a different address), you have the option of adding a mailing address or post office box as well if you prefer to get your mail somewhere else.
7. When you put in the name of the organization, remember to add *Inc* or *Corp* if that is part of your organization name (but leave off the period at the end).
8. On the screen that says *Tell us more about the Nonprofit/Tax-Exempt Organization,* most or all the answers will be *NO*. If you click on employees, even though you don't currently have employees, IRS will code your EIN to expect employee reports from you. If you are just starting, you might want to check

NO for everything. Once you get employees, you can file the necessary reports with IRS.

The next screen will ask you to specify your type of services (retail, insurance, health care, transportation, etc.). Just check *Other* at the bottom. On the next page, choose *Other* again and enter about five words or less to explain your purpose briefly. Some examples that will fit include:

- Tangible assistance to the needy
- Orphan care in Africa
- Job training for veterans
- Assist elderly and handicapped
- Drug prevention and awareness
- After-school childrens programs (no apostrophe in children's, IRS doesn't allow punctuation except for hyphen and ampersand)
- Support system for cancer patients

When asked how you want to receive your EIN, click on **Receive letter online**. The next screen will be a review of all information you submitted. Proofread the name, address, and other information before submitting. If you made a mistake such as forgetting *Inc* or *Corp*, your only choice is to start over. There is a button at the top right of the screen to start a new EIN. That is how you start over before the first EIN is issued in error. If there are no errors, click to submit and your EIN will come up on the screen.

WRITE DOWN THE NUMBER before touching anything else on your computer! It is a nine-digit number that starts with two digits followed by a dash, then seven more digits. Why write it down before touching anything? Sometimes, when you click on the link to give you the letter, the screen blinks and the EIN is gone. If that happens, you have to call IRS at (800) 829-4933 and ask them for the Tax ID number. Best to write it down just in case. Then click to get the letter and save it to your computer. If you do it correctly, it will be Form CP 575 E.

Although uncommon, there are several reasons your EIN might not process online. When that happens, you will get an error code. Here are some common error codes and what they normally mean:

- **Code 101**: Normally means the name or an extremely similar name is already in use in your state. In that case, call IRS (the number will appear on the screen) or call (800) 829-4933 to make sure someone else on the board didn't already get the EIN and forget to tell you, or that you didn't get it earlier and forgot about it because some time has gone by since then.

  If you did the name availability search from the previous chapter and the name was available, then you shouldn't encounter Code 101. However, what sometimes happens is that an organization years ago got an EIN in the same state for the same name, then closed up shop and dissolved with the state, but forgot to tell IRS that they don't exist anymore. In that case, go ahead and file your state incorporation and send IRS a copy of the approval with the mail-in or fax-in EIN request (IRS Form SS-4). IRS will issue an EIN for your organization even though another exists for the same name in the same state at some time in the past. If the state is willing to approve the name, IRS will also approve it. If all else fails, tweak the name a little and apply with a slightly different name.
- Codes 102, 103, 105, and 108. These codes normally mean the name and social do not match IRS records. Check your social security card or get someone else on the board to apply for the EIN.
- Codes 109, 110, 112, and 113. These codes normally mean technical problems at IRS or too many people applying for EINs at the same time. Try later.
- Code 114 means you already received one EIN that day with that social and you are limited to one per day. Try again tomorrow or get someone else on the board to use their social to apply. If you made a mistake and started over, it could mean that for some reason, IRS processed the first request and the number was issued. In that case, call IRS and ask to be sure.

2. THE MAIL-IN or FAX-IN OPTION

If you do not want to or cannot get your EIN online, you can fill out and mail or fax IRS Form SS-4. You can do an internet search for the form and fill it out online (or print and write it in by hand), and mail to:

>Internal Revenue Service Center
>ATTN: EIN Operation
>Cincinnati, Ohio 45999

You can fax the completed form to (855) 641-6935.

If you fax the form, IRS will fax the FEIN back to the fax number you provided on the SS-4. It normally takes 4 – 5 days. If you mail in the form, the EIN will come back in the mail in about 2 – 3 weeks. If you fax in but do not give a fax number to respond, IRS will mail the EIN in 2 – 3 weeks.

SOME TIPS TO MAKE FORM SS-4 EASY:

Item 9a: Check *Other Nonprofit Organization (specify)*: _____.
    On the line, give a brief description of the purpose or write *Public Charity*.
Item 9b: Put in your state even though you may not already be incorporated.
Item 10: Check *Started a new business*.
Item 11: Use today's date or if you are already incorporated, the incorporation date from the state.
Item 12: The normal answer is 12 (which means the twelfth month or December 31) for the end of the fiscal year. Some educational organizations use June 30 or July 31, but then their tax returns are due near Thanksgiving or right before Christmas, and that puts a damper on the holidays to stop and file nonprofit tax returns, even though nonprofits do not owe any taxes. They still have to file.

Item 13: Normally blank.
Item 14: Normally is not checked.
Item 15: N/A
Item 16: Other: Public Charity.
Item 17: Add a *brief* mission, a few words that describe your purpose, but don't make it too narrow in case you decide to expand it later. *Assist the homeless* is preferable to *Give blankets to homeless on nights when temperatures go below 28 degrees*. Why? Because you might want to also give them hot soup or a place to take a shower, and maybe in ten years you will decide to add some job training to help them get off the street.
Item 18: No. The applicant is the nonprofit, not you personally. No matter how many EINs you have, the organization has none, so the answer is *NO*.

WHAT IF YOU MADE A MISTAKE ON THE FEIN?

If you made a mistake on the FEIN, you need to correct it with IRS. For address errors, use *IRS Form 8822-B, Change of Address or Responsible Party – Business*. You also use this form if the responsible party for the organization changes, for example, if the founding person steps off the board and leaves the organization.

If you forgot to add *Inc.* or *Corp.*, or had a typo in spelling, mail or fax a letter to the EIN section at IRS requesting they correct it. There is no standard form, so just send a letter. Give them the information as it appears on the FEIN CP 575 E form (or another form number if you checked the wrong box instead of *Other Nonprofit/Tax-Exempt Organization*), and then give them the corrected information. Here is the address to use for recently issued EINs that need corrections:

Internal Revenue Service
Stop 343G
Cincinnati, OH 45999
Fax Number: 859-669-5760.

A letter may look something like this:

Organization Name (old name) Date
C/O Your Name
Address
City ST Zip

Internal Revenue Service
Stop 343G
Cincinnati, OH 45999
Fax: (859) 669-5760

RE: Change to FEIN _____

Dear Sir/Ma'am,

We made a mistake when we applied for the organization FEIN. We forgot to include the state's mandatory requirement of Inc. at the end of the organization name. The correct name should be:

                List new name here

Please change our name on your records so that they match the state's records.

Thank you,

Your Name
President (or other office you hold)
Phone Number

IRS will not send a letter acknowledging that they made the change, they will just update your records.

THE CLOCK STARTS TICKING

Once an EIN is issued for a nonprofit, the clock starts ticking for tax returns. You must file a tax return with IRS for the nonprofit (even if you have no revenues or expenses) within 4 ½ months of the fiscal year end. For organizations that have December 31 fiscal year end, that means the first nonprofit tax return is due by May 15 of the following year. You do not need 501(c)(3) status to be obligated to file taxes; you just need to be registered with the state as a nonprofit. You file taxes because you are a nonprofit, not because you have 501(c)(3) tax-exempt status with IRS. Either way, you must file an information tax return for the nonprofit every year unless you are a church.

If there is a time gap between getting the EIN and incorporating with the state, the state effective date will start the clock ticking for tax returns. For example, suppose you got your FEIN in December of one year but did not file the state incorporation until January of the next year. The official start date of the corporation would be January, and that is when the clock started ticking for tax returns. In this example, you would get an extra year before the first tax return is due.

If for some reason you change your mind, or things do not work out, you are not in trouble with IRS if you get the number and never use it. Just let them know you are closing the EIN account.

HOW TO CLOSE AN FEIN ACCOUNT:

If you were issued an FEIN and intended to set up a nonprofit corporation, but you never got around to starting, you can send a letter to IRS asking them to close the FEIN account. You must tell them why, and give them the FEIN number, the legal name of the organization, and the mailing address. If you have a copy of the EIN paperwork, send a copy with the request.

Send to:
>
> Internal Revenue Service
> Attn: EO Entity
> Mail Stop 6273
> Ogden, UT 84201

You may fax the request to (855) 214-7520.

You now have several steps out of the way. The next item on your agenda is to create a strong mission statement. More about that in the next chapter.

CHAPTER 7

DEVELOP A STRONG MISSION STATEMENT

"You can only overcome rejection when your goals are more important than approval."

—MIKE MURDOCK

DEFINE THE MISSION YOU ARE ON

Your organization needs a mission statement. If you are the founder(s), you know better than anyone the message you want to convey about your organization. You're on a mission, and your mission statement should reflect your passion. In a sentence or two, what is that mission that motivates you? Your answer should be active, short, inspiring, and cause people to remember you. Erica Olsen said that if your mission statement would make a great t-shirt, it is probably a good one.

> YOU'RE ON A MISSION, AND YOUR MISSION STATEMENT SHOULD REFLECT YOUR PASSION.

LEARN FROM OTHERS

To help you find the right words to express the mission of your organization, I have located a dozen of the best written U. S. nonprofit mission statements for you to study. Notice the statements that get your attention, inspire you, make you want to know more, or match your pre-existing perception of the organization.

> *American Diabetes Association:* To prevent and cure diabetes and to improve the lives of all people affected by diabetes.
> *AmeriCares Foundation*: In times of epic disaster or daily struggle, we deliver medical and humanitarian aid to people in need worldwide.
> *Feed the Children*: Delivers food, medicine, clothing and other necessities to individuals, children and families who lack these essentials due to famine, war, poverty or natural disaster.
> *Good360*: Fulfill the needs of nonprofits with corporate product donations.
> *Habitat for Humanity International*: Seeking to put God's love into action, Habitat for Humanity brings people together to build homes, communities and hope.
> *Humane Society of the United States*: Celebrating Animals, Confronting Cruelty.
> *Leukemia and Lymphoma Society*: Cure leukemia, lymphoma, Hodgkin's disease and myeloma, and improve the quality of life of patients and their families.
> *Make a Wish Foundation of America*: We grant the wishes of children with life-threatening medical conditions to enrich the human experience with hope, strength and joy.
> *National Multiple Sclerosis Society*: We mobilize people and resources to drive research for a cure and to address the challenges of everyone affected by MS.
> *Smile Train*: Provide a child born with a cleft the same opportunities in life as a child born without a cleft.

World Wildlife Federation: Protecting the future of nature.

Wycliffe Bible Translators: To see a Bible translation program in progress in every language still needing one by 2025.

NOW IT'S YOUR TURN

Now it is time to develop your mission statement. Here are some guidelines to add pizzazz:

- Keep it short: 6–15 words are normally sufficient. Use active tense: *We feed hungry kids!* is better than *We strive to eliminate hunger in children.*
- Try your mission statement out on others of different ages and get input.
- Avoid jargon and formal language. Make it so clear a child can understand what is exciting about what you do. Jargon and formal language do not convey your enthusiasm. If in doubt, ask a kid.
- Be specific about the population you serve, but do not box yourself in so that you cannot expand your reach later. Chances are you are not going to eradicate AIDS from the planet, but you can provide antiretroviral medication to Ethiopia's poor. You may provide computers to the poor now, but what about the next latest, greatest, better-than-computers invention? You might want to say *technology* instead of *computers*, so you don't limit yourself down the road.
- Do away with theoretical, scholarly, or academic mission statements.
- Leave out words that water down the effectiveness of your organization.

> BE SPECIFIC ABOUT THE POPULATION YOU SERVE, BUT DO NOT BOX YOURSELF IN SO THAT YOU CANNOT EXPAND YOUR REACH LATER.

Here are a few that you should avoid:

Try	Endeavor
Attempt	Strive
Aim	Pursue
Help	Undertake
Influence	

Instead, use powerful words like these:

Prevent	Mobilize
Abolish	Reduce
Confront	Save
Connect	Solve
Eliminate	Transform
Increase	Improve

- Identify the problem you target, and the solution you provide.
- Use clear, concise, brief, and positive terms to paint a picture of the mission you are on.

You can always change or update your mission statement later if necessary. It doesn't have to be perfect or carved in stone. For now, write it and move on. Notice the missions above do not contain the details of how the organization will operate. The day-to-day logistics of operation must be ironed out by the board of directors; the mission is the *end result* you want from the efforts you make and the logistical considerations you tackle.

> YOU CAN ALWAYS CHANGE OR UPDATE YOUR MISSION STATEMENT LATER IF NECESSARY.

In the next chapter, you'll learn how to form your board of directors.

CHAPTER 8

FORM A BOARD OF DIRECTORS

"Opportunity is missed by most people because it is dressed in overalls and looks like work."

—THOMAS EDISON

NOT SHAREHOLDERS, BUT STAKEHOLDERS

The Board of Directors is the governing body of a nonprofit. Every officer of the board is a board director, but not every board director has to be an officer. Boards normally have a president, vice president (can have more than one covering different areas such as communications or programs), secretary, and treasurer as officers, and other board members are simply called board members or board directors (those terms are synonymous).

THE BOARD OF DIRECTORS IS THE GOVERNING BODY OF A NONPROFIT.

If you are not on the Board of Directors, you have no authority in guiding the organization. Board members are not the managers; management answers to the board of directors. In profit corporations, board members are responsible to the owners (the stockholders). A nonprofit organization is not owned, so board members answer to:

- The public
- The government
- Their supporters
- The people the organization serves

For-profit corporations are concerned mostly about the bottom line – the money. However, in a nonprofit atmosphere, board members are not shareholders; they are stakeholders. They have a stake in the success of the nonprofit that has little to do with finance.

QUALIFIED AND WILLING

It is a privilege to be on a nonprofit board of directors, and members should be selected based on qualifications and willingness to serve. They don't need great business acumen or experience but should have good judgment and common sense. The board should be a mix of visionaries and practical souls so that a balance exists, although harmony may not be a 24/7 accomplishment when you put dreamers and realists together. Board members should be matched to board positions that most effectively utilize their skills and talents.

ACCOUNTANT OR ATTORNEY AS BOARD MEMBER?

There are arguments for and against having an accountant or attorney on the board. If you choose to include either, make sure your motives are not so that you can get free expertise. That is unfair to the board member and to the organization. Better to ask them for pro bono or reduced-price services and select board members who have a heart for the organization's mission.

HOW MANY BOARD MEMBERS?

IRS does not specifically establish a set number of board members, but too few or too unqualified can cause delays and questions during the processing phase of your 501(c)(3) application. Relationships are also an important component of board formation. Relatives (by blood or marriage) should hold less than 50% of the vote on a board of directors for a public charity. Foundations can have all family members, but foundations operate with many more limitations than public charities and have lots more paperwork to do.

As a minimum, three board members who are not related, and if two are related, then five board members are needed to pass IRS scrutiny. There is no maximum number of board members. There should be as many as are needed to govern the organization. In addition, IRS monitors whether board members are independent members who do not benefit financially from the organization while making board decisions.

In addition to IRS codes, every state has nonprofit business statutes that spell out the minimum number of directors on the board, and the positions of those directors. None require more than a minimum of three except New Hampshire which requires five.

START SMALL

To meet the requirements of IRS, you need at least three board members. To start with, you might do well to keep the number of board members to a minimum. It takes less initial paperwork, fewer biographies, and fewer signatures to get everything up and running. The fewer the board members, the fewer people IRS will have to scrutinize. You can add more board members after starting the organization. You might want to consider having an odd number of board members so that there is no tie when voting.

> THE FEWER THE BOARD MEMBERS, THE FEWER PEOPLE IRS WILL HAVE TO SCRUTINIZE.

HOW TO ADD BOARD MEMBERS

You get to pick who is on the initial board. Consider approaching potential board members to be *interim* (temporary) board members until the first election which is normally held at the beginning of a new fiscal year. That way, if they don't work out, they are only in your hair for a short time. To add members later, simply vote in new board members at a board meeting. Document the vote in the board meeting minutes.

HOW TO REMOVE BOARD MEMBERS

When you want to get someone off the board, you can address it with the person one-on-one and ask them to resign. If they refuse, you bring it to a vote at a board meeting, whether a regular meeting or one called specifically to vote on removing the board member. Your bylaws tell what percentage of the board must vote for different areas, and they should tell what the required percentage is to remove a board member with or without cause. Suppose the percentage is 75%. That means that if there are three board members total, and two vote to remove a member, that only equals 67% and is not enough to vote the person off the board if they refuse to go willingly. However, if you have four members on the board and three vote for removal, that is 75% and the person causing the problem is gone. Moral of the story: Be very careful who you put on the board. People who are stubborn, argumentative, arrogant, holier-than-thou, always want to be in charge, always know best, or want everything their way don't belong on your board. If you need them to fill a slot to help you get the organization started, make them interim (temporary) board members with the understanding that you only need them to serve on your board until the next election of members and then they are free to go with your thanks and gratitude for their selfless. Instead, you can also ask them to be an advisor to the board. Advisors have no voting rights and attend board meetings upon your invitation only.

> BE VERY CAREFUL WHO YOU PUT ON THE BOARD.

If a problem develops with a member who is not an *interim* director, add some new people to the board before trying to vote the undesirable person out, so you have a high enough percentage to eliminate them from your board. If the troubling person is an officer such as president, there is a way to lessen their influence. During the annual election, the board might vote in a different member to take that officer position and reduce the troublemaker to a regular board position. That would help get the message across that you want them to go away, and might make them mad enough to leave on their own. If they don't, you should know that every board member has one vote regardless of position. The president gets one vote, and a regular board member gets one vote. Each vote has the same weight when tallying up the total vote.

CONVERSATIONS WITH IRS ABOUT YOU GETTING VOTED OFF THE BOARD

Many clients have asked me how to make sure they never get voted off the board. That is a valid concern. If you are going to put your sweat into building an organization, you don't want to lose it. Nonprofits are not owned, and there is a possibility that you could be voted off the board. As a public charity, you cannot make your position a forever carved-in-stone appointment.

One specific client comes to mind, a religious woman in a male-dominated denomination. She was starting a religious school for children and paid for everything out of her pocket to get it started and did most of the work herself to get it going. Sound familiar? She had legitimate concerns that once it was up and running that the male board members would vote her out. It had happened before in other situations she knew about, and she was just plain worried. So, I posed the question of what to do to IRS on her behalf. The answer made all the sense in the world, and I have used it since.

The IRS agent confirmed that board members are not restricted to the same location as the nonprofit. You can have an organization in one state, and all your board members can be in other states (or other countries

> THE IRS AGENT CONFIRMED THAT BOARD MEMBERS ARE NOT RESTRICTED TO THE SAME LOCATION AS THE NONPROFIT.

if you have an international mission). They can be friends, acquaintances, college roommates, old business contacts, and distant relatives such as aunts, uncles, and cousins. You can also have family members but stay under 50% total voting power to stay off IRS radar.

Every state allows board meetings held by technology such as Skype, GoToMeeting, Google Hangouts, or conference calls as long as everyone can hear everyone else, and all have the capacity to contribute to the meeting. Not much chance of people in other states (or countries) voting you off the board.

To make sure I was given good counsel, I called IRS back two more times and talked with two other agents who gave me the same answer.

MEMBER TRAITS AND QUALITIES

Regardless of the position held by the board member, there are some defining traits and qualities that are essential to successful governance of a nonprofit organization:

- Ethical behavior and integrity
- No conflicts of interest
- Willingness to speak up and voice an opinion (even if unpopular)
- Inclination to cooperate and compromise when necessary
- Eagerness to invest the time necessary to succeed

Below are basic job descriptions for the most common positions on the Board of Directors. You can tailor the job descriptions to whatever your organization needs from the board members. You can call the positions whatever you want; you are not limited to the titles given.

President (or Chairman) of the Board

Chairman sounds more like a title for a profit corporation, so President is often used for nonprofit corporations. Helpful attributes include:

- Leadership skills
- Earned respect of board members
- Good communication skills
- Ability to make hard calls when difficult decisions must be made
- Willingness to delegate

If you are the founder and you have those qualifications, then consider making yourself the initial President of the Board of Directors. You may be the most qualified person for the job.

A sample job description might be:

The President of the Board represents the organization as ambassador to the community; presides over the affairs of the board and assists in setting agendas for board meetings; coordinates establishment of committees, assignments, and execution of tasks; steers board selection of an Executive Director; leads strategic planning and fundraising efforts; recruits and trains new board members; and delegates responsibility and authority to accomplish the goals of the organization.

Vice President (or Vice Chairman) of the Board

The Vice President is sometimes the successor to the President, a President in training, or President-elect. The corporate bylaws should reflect whether that is the case. Helpful attributes for Vice President are the same as for the President.

A sample job description might be:

> *The Vice President of the Board acts as the President when the President is not available. He or she assists the President in executing duties and performs other duties as assigned by the Board.*

Secretary of the Board

The Secretary of the Board is the communication and record keeping member of the Board of Directors. He or she should be familiar with the mission and vision of the organization, the Articles of Incorporation, and the bylaws. Helpful attributes include an aptitude for organization, writing abilities, and communication competence.

A sample job description might be:

> *The Secretary of the Board maintains records of all Board actions; prepares and distributes meeting minutes; safeguards all corporation records; presides over meetings in the absence of the President and Vice President; and performs other duties as assigned by the Board.*

Treasurer (or Chief Financial Officer, CFO) of the Board

The Treasurer or CFO of the Board is the go-to person for financial questions in an organization. He or she must be above reproach with integrity, and maintain transparency in performing the duties of the office. Helpful attributes for Treasurer include critical thinking skills, analytical ability, and willingness to learn financial accounting principles as they relate to nonprofit organizations. The Treasurer does not have to actually prepare financial reports, but must make sure they get done.

A sample job description might be:

> *The Treasurer of the Board coordinates and ensures financial stewardship and financial well-being of the organization; manages finances; ensures timely and accurate filing of financial reports to IRS and state agencies; presents annual budgets for board approval; reviews annual audits; signs and deposits checks; and performs other duties as assigned by the Board.*

Board Member or Board Director

Not every member of the Board of Directors needs to hold a title to an office, but all officers are directors. In other words, whether a board member holds an office or not, they are still board directors. *Board member* and *board director* mean the same thing. All positions are important and add to the effective governance of a nonprofit organization. Each board member should be a volunteer who is committed to the mission of the organization. This is a person who is willing to make time and actively participate in board meetings, fundraising activities, and public events involving the organization. In addition to investing time, board members should also be willing to invest money. Each member should have a copy of the organization's conflict of interest policy and sign a disclosure form annually.

A sample job description might be:

> *Board Members attend regularly scheduled board meetings; actively participate in decision making, considering the best interest of the organization; maintain integrity in use of resources; adhere to the letter and intent of regulatory guidance; establish and carry out planning, policies, fundraising, and budgeting; and evaluate the Executive Director's (if there is one) performance and compensation annually.*

SHOULD WE HAVE AN EXECUTIVE DIRECTOR?

Most new organizations do not need a paid program director, executive director, or someone with a similar job title. Paid employees work for and report to the Board of Directors. Once the organization grows big enough to need a program director, then is the time to get to work finding the best fit for the position. So, how do you do that?

Start by thinking about what the requirements would be for a paid position to run your program. Have the board members do some research between board meetings. They will need to create the job description, determine the hours, and set the pay based on qualifications needed and the organization's budget. When determining compensation, you need to make sure it is reasonable for the services performed, and comparable to other nonprofits of similar size and mission.

Once you have some parameters to work within, discuss the details at a board meeting. When the details are ironed out, someone makes a motion to hire a program director (by whatever name you come up with), approve the job description, confirm the hours and pay, and set a start date for the position. Then you begin seeking candidates to fill the position.

> START BY THINKING ABOUT WHAT THE REQUIREMENTS WOULD BE FOR A PAID POSITION TO RUN YOUR PROGRAM.

If someone on your board turns out to be the best qualified for the job, that is not an issue. As long as the pay is reasonable and the work is actually being performed, go ahead and hire that person. However, board members cannot vote to hire themselves; it is a conflict of interest. Make the person leave the room while the rest of the board votes to hire them (even if that turns out to be you). It is acceptable for a board member to also be a paid director, although I don't recommend it until the organization has 501(c)(3) approval (paperwork is simpler if you wait) and is financially able to support the position. If you hire a board member as the program director, that member doesn't get paid to go to board meetings; he or she gets paid to run the organization's programs under board supervision. Also, be aware of the percentages spent on salaries and benefits compared to the overall budget. If the organization takes in $50,000 a year and pays out $40,000 to the program director, that could be a huge red flag at IRS depending on the mission. If the program is an after-school volunteer tutoring program, RED FLAG! If the program is counseling veterans with PTSD and the program director is a trained psychologist or therapist who will be working with veterans, then there is no red flag.

With your board of directors now in place, you are ready to learn about incorporation.

CHAPTER 9

CRASH COURSE ON INCORPORATION

*"Nothing will ever be attempted,
if all possible objections must first be overcome."*

—SAMUEL JACKSON

THE BIRTH OF AN ORGANIZATION

When a child is born, a vital record of that birth is created in the state in which the child was born – it's called the *Birth Certificate*. It's recorded by the state, and it registers the presence of a new little person. The certificate documents who the parents are, where and when the child was born, and other important information verifying the child's existence. The child is given a name, and in some cases, a suffix (such as Jr. or III) that further identifies the child. The child's origin is declared, such as Caucasian, Hispanic, or Native American. The parents complete the paperwork and the hospital sends it to the bureau of vital records (by whatever name the state calls that department), and a birth certificate is created.

When a nonprofit corporation is born, a vital record of that birth is created in the state in which the organization was born – it's normally called the *Articles of Incorporation*. It is recorded by the state, and it registers the presence of a new organization. The paperwork declares who the parents are (the incorporators), where and when the organization was born, and other vital information verifying the organization's existence. The nonprofit is given a name, and in some cases, a suffix (such as Inc. or Corp.) that further identifies the organization. The nonprofit's origin is declared, such as Public Benefit, Mutual Benefit, or Religious. The incorporator completes the paperwork and sends it to the state's Corporations Division, and a *business birth certificate* (figuratively speaking) is created.

WHEN A NONPROFIT CORPORATION IS BORN, A VITAL RECORD OF THAT BIRTH IS CREATED IN THE STATE IN WHICH THE ORGANIZATION WAS BORN – IT'S NORMALLY CALLED THE **ARTICLES OF INCORPORATION**.

A MATTER OF PUBLIC RECORD

A birth certificate is a public record in the sense that if you are related and have a need to know, you can get a copy. The analogy differs when compared to a nonprofit corporation. Incorporation records are public records and as such are available to the public. Anyone wishing access is allowed to see, read, and have a copy of your nonprofit's birth certificate. For this reason, it's a good idea to leave out social security numbers and other personal identifiers in the documents you file.

Public charitable foundations, funds, community chests, and some trusts may also be eligible for 501(c) (3) status under certain circumstances, if they exist for charitable purposes. Their filing requirements are similar to nonprofit corporations, but their documents have different names, such as *Articles of Association* instead of *Articles of Incorporation*. Incorporation provides more legal protection for officers than unincorporated organizations.

ANYONE WISHING ACCESS IS ALLOWED TO SEE, READ, AND HAVE A COPY OF YOUR NONPROFIT'S BIRTH CERTIFICATE.

TYPES OF NONPROFITS

To establish a vital record with your state and IRS, you must decide the origin or type of organization because it has far-reaching consequences for 501(c)(3) status. There are three broad categories of nonprofits:

Public Benefit

A public benefit organization is normally a charity with a charitable mission, and IRS recognizes this type of organization for 501(c)(3) tax-exempt status. A public benefit corporation cannot be established to help just one organization (such as a specific orphanage) or individual (such as a particular orphan) but must benefit a class of people or group of organizations (such as potentially benefiting any orphan or orphanage in Mexico). You can start small by initially benefiting one or two specific orphanages, but must allow for helping others in the same category or class. If your nonprofit benefits only one organization or a defined finite group of people who can be identified by name (such as a family), it is a private foundation, not a public benefit corporation.

A PUBLIC BENEFIT ORGANIZATION IS NORMALLY A CHARITY WITH A CHARITABLE MISSION.

This differentiation does not mean that your public charity cannot help an individual or a family, but it does mean that you cannot limit your efforts in establishing a nonprofit to specific people or families, you must leave room to grow and add people or families whose names you do not know yet.

Public benefit organizations handling less than $5,000 per year are automatically exempt and do not need to file for 501(c)(3) tax-exempt status until they reach the $5,000 revenue level in a given fiscal year. Regardless of revenues, *all* nonprofits except churches must file annual nonprofit tax returns, even if they have no income or expenses.

Feed the Children and *United Way* are examples of Public Benefit nonprofits.

Mutual Benefit

A mutual benefit nonprofit exists to benefit members of a group. It is similar to a club. People pay membership fees or join the group, and assets are distributed among the members if the organization dissolves. IRS does not normally give 501(c) (3) status to mutual benefit organizations because they serve their members, not the public. Examples are an electric cooperative association or the local chapter of the *Veterans of Foreign Wars*. They are nonprofits, but not 501(c) (3) tax-exempt nonprofits.

Religious

There are two kinds of religious nonprofits: denominational churches and other religious organizations.

Denominational churches never have to file for 501(c) (3) tax-exempt status because they are automatically exempt, and donations are automatically deductible. However, once a church gets twenty-five or more members (not attendees, actual members who have met the membership requirements and been accepted as church members), they normally apply for 501(c) (3) status to soothe the anxieties of their tithers who worry that IRS might turn down their tax deductions. When that time arrives, denominational churches must jump through a lot of hoops to get church status, but it is worth the effort because once church status is granted, the church never has to file tax returns again and the congregation can rest assured that their tithes and offerings are tax deductible. IRS can audit a church based on complaints, but other than that, IRS has little to do with approved churches once they give the stamp of approval. That may be why IRS makes churches answer to fourteen extra requirements that other nonprofits do not have.

Nondenominational churches, evangelical ministries, and other religious nonprofits are eligible for 501(c) (3) status from IRS, but they must file tax returns every year.

Samaritan's Purse is an example of a religious nonprofit, and *World Vision* is an example of a church (yes, they started as a church).

FOREIGN VS. DOMESTIC CORPORATION

To conduct nonprofit business in other states, you must first be recognized as a nonprofit entity in your own state by filing an incorporation document such as *Articles of Incorporation*, which gets you a business birth certificate, figuratively speaking. Then you can apply to the Corporations Division in other states as a *foreign* nonprofit corporation for recognition and approval to conduct nonprofit business in their state. The application you complete results in a *Certificate of Authority* from the other state saying you can do business in their state, too. You are not incorporating in other states, you only have one business birth certificate, but you can move around to other states and operate in them. You will always be incorporated in the state in which your organization was born. If you decide to incorporate in another state instead of getting a Certificate of Authority to operate in that state, you have to start from scratch and set up a new organization. Incorporations do not transfer from one state to another, and if you incorporate in a new state, you must file for 501(c) (3) again with IRS for the new incorporation.

Foreign does not mean foreign country, it means from outside the state boundaries; *domestic* means inside the state boundaries. You are a domestic corporation in your home state, and a foreign corporation in all other states. It normally costs more to be registered as a foreign nonprofit corporation than a domestic nonprofit in a state. Outsiders usually get charged more.

Each state has its own requirements, fees, and forms for Certificate of Authority. Most states require proof that you are approved, and that your organization is doing reputable business in your home state. This requirement is usually met by providing a recently certified copy of your state's *Certificate of Good Standing, Certificate of Existence, Certificate of Fact* (Texas), or similar state document. It is a piece of paper provided by your Corporations Division that you pay to have certified, usually not more than 60 days prior to applying to another state for approval to conduct business. If the good standing paperwork gets too old, you have to pay to get another copy certified with a more recent date.

Getting a Certificate of Authority to operate in a state is not the same thing as being approved to do fundraising in that state. Those are two separate functions. Thirty-eight states and District of Columbia have charitable registration. You pay a fee, file a form, provide requested copies of documents, and you are allowed to raise funds once approved, except in Illinois. They run six to twelve months behind on processing charitable registration (I am not making it up!), so you can start raising funds in good faith as soon as you mail the registration to Illinois. Send it with tracking, so you have proof of the date you sent it.

WHAT IF I MOVE OFTEN? WHAT HAPPENS TO THE NONPROFIT?

Pick the state to incorporate in carefully. If you move around a lot, Delaware is friendly to nonprofits and is a good choice. Delaware does not have charitable registration, so that is a plus. Many corporations register in Delaware and operate elsewhere because it is easy to get registered and stay compliant without a bunch of ongoing paperwork like California has. You can register in Delaware and get a Certificate of Authority for the state you live in. Then when you move, get a Certificate of Authority for the new state, and your 501(c)(3) remains in force. You can actually do that in any state, but Delaware is often picked as the home state because it has good laws to attract businesses.

REQUIREMENT FOR REGISTERED AGENT

To do business as either a domestic or a foreign nonprofit corporation, you must have a *registered agent*. This is a person or business in the state in which you want to conduct business who agrees to be the eyes and ears for the nonprofit. The registered agent's purpose is to give the Corporations Division a contact person with a street address (as opposed to a post office box) inside the state lines who will receive official mail, handle complaints, answer telephone inquiries from state offices, and just generally be the go-to person or company on behalf of your nonprofit. Don't worry, if the state asks a question the registered agent cannot answer, they have time to contact you and get the answer.

You can be the registered agent for your organization in your state if you are willing to be the face and voice behind the corporate name and mission. The registered agent can be a commercial agent or a non-commerical agent. It can be an individual or organization willing to be your representative, or it can be a company for hire who is approved by the state to represent other organizations.

To find a commercial registered agent, you can do an internet search for registered agent and the state, or you can call the Corporation Division and ask for a list of approved registered agents in the state. If you get Certificates of Authority to operate in all 50 states, you must have registered agents in all those states. Hopefully, you will have friends or family in many of the states who are willing to be your registered agents, so you don't have to hire so many commercial registered agents and pay them every year.

REQUIRED STATEMENTS FOR IRS 501(C) (3) APPROVAL

The exact wording of your incorporation document is not critical except for a few required statements that if missing, will cause your application for 501(c) (3) status to be rejected. If IRS *suggests* something, it is a good idea to follow the suggestion. Here is the IRS *suggested* wording to meet their required language and statements:

Benefit Statement (IRS will not turn down your incorporation if you don't include this, but they suggest that you include it):

> *No part of the net earnings of the corporation shall inure to the benefit, or be distributable to its members, trustees, officers, or other private persons, except that the corporation shall be authorized and empowered*

to pay reasonable compensation for services rendered and to make payments and distributions in furtherance of its tax-exempt purposes.

No substantial part of the activities of the corporation shall be the carrying on of propaganda, or otherwise attempting to influence legislation, and the corporation shall not participate in, or intervene in (including the publishing or distribution of statements) any political campaign on behalf of or in opposition to any candidate for public office.

Notwithstanding any other provision of these articles, the corporation shall not carry on any other activities not permitted to be carried on (a) by a corporation exempt from federal income tax under Section 501(c) (3) of the Internal Revenue Code, or the corresponding section of any future federal tax code, or (b) by a corporation, contributions to which are deductible under Section 170(c) (2) of the Internal Revenue Code, or the corresponding section of any future federal tax code.

Purpose Statement (IRS will turn down your incorporation without this statement):

Said Corporation is organized exclusively for charitable, religious, educational, and scientific purposes, including, for such purposes, the making of distributions to organizations that qualify as exempt organizations under Section 501(c) (3) of the Internal Revenue Code, or the corresponding section of any future federal tax code.

Dissolution Statement (IRS will turn down your incorporation without the first sentence, but suggests you include the second sentence as well, even though it sounds like a bunch of legal mumbo-jumbo):

Upon the dissolution of the corporation, assets shall be distributed for one or more exempt purposes within the meaning of Section 501(c) (3) of the Internal Revenue Code, or corresponding section of any future federal tax code, or shall be distributed to the federal government, or to a state or local government, for a public purpose.

Any such assets not so disposed of shall be disposed of by a Court of Competent Jurisdiction of the county in which the principal office of the corporation is then located, exclusively for such purposes or to such organization or organizations as said Court shall determine which are organized and operated exclusively for such purposes.

INFORMATION FOR INCORPORATION

There is some relatively constant information across states that should be included in the incorporation document. Every state requires some form of the following:

- Name of the corporation
- Type of corporation: public benefit, mutual benefit, or religious
- Duration (normally perpetual)
- Street address and mailing address of the initial registered office and the name of the initial registered agent
- The name of the incorporator(s)
- The purpose and dissolution statements (not required by the state, but required by IRS, and benefit statement suggested by IRS)
- Whether the corporation has members. Most nonprofits DO NOT have members. Organizations are either run by the Board or Directors or by the membership. The question about members means membership. Board members do not constitute membership. It is usually an either/or choice.
- Who will manage the affairs of the corporation? (normally the Board of Directors)
- The number of directors (make sure you include the required positions for your state)
- The term and manner of election of directors (you can say that they will be as provided or described in the Bylaws)
- That the Articles can be amended by the Board of Directors in the manner provided by the Bylaws (unless you want to include those details in the incorporation documents)

- Articles to protect directors and officers from lawsuits (optional)
- A statement that the corporation may purchase general comprehensive liability insurance covering the board members and officers in the performance of their duties (optional)
- An affirmation that all information is true and correct, and execution by signature(s) by the incorporator(s) on a specific date

Now that you know bits and pieces about incorporation, let's get your nonprofit incorporation paperwork done.

CHAPTER 10

LET'S INCORPORATE AND STAY COMPLIANT!

*It's one thing to talk about what is wrong -
It's another to actually do something about it.*

—STEVE WOOD, NEW BRAUNFELS, TEXAS

In addition to IRS codes, every state has nonprofit business statutes that spell out the minimum number of directors on the board, and the positions of those directors. Below are your statute and the board composition guidelines:

- Statute: Corporate Code, Chapter 317A of the Minnesota Statutes
- Minimum Board Members: 3
- Required Offices: President, Secretary, Treasurer

*If you start with 3 members (which meets IRS minimum), you can have President, Vice President, and one person can be Secretary and Treasurer simultaneously.

WHAT YOU DO TO GET INCORPORATED

Incorporation in Minnesota costs either $70 to mail in, or $90 to file online or walk in. You have two choices to incorporate in Minnesota:

1. File online (with attachment below containing IRS clauses)
2. Complete your own Articles of Incorporation (example later in this chapter).

> ***NOTE:** *DO NOT* use the state's form to mail in. It does not contain the required IRS clauses to qualify for 501(c)(3) tax exempt status.

1. FILE ONLINE

Before you start, type up your attachment or go to *www.doyourownnonprofit.com* and download it. Have it ready for the filing process. Save it as a PDF. You can easily set up an online account and incorporate in Minnesota in less than 30 minutes.

Here is what you do:

1. Go to *https://mblsportal.sos.state.mn.us/Account/Register*
2. Set up an account
3. Once logged in, scroll down to Nonprofit Corporation (domestic)
4. Professional Status and Services: No
5. Do the Name Search. Then under Name Search, click on *File Nonprofit Corporation*
6. Answer the questions until you get to the one that says *Add an Attachment*
7. Upload your attachment that contains this information (remember to fill in the two blanks before uploading):

ADDITIONAL ARTICLES

Purpose

[Enter Corporation name] is a nonprofit corporation organized exclusively for charitable, religious, educational, and scientific purposes, including, for such purposes, the making of distributions to organizations that qualify as exempt organizations, under Section 501 (c)(3) of the Internal Revenue Code, or the corresponding section of any future federal tax code.

The Corporation's mission is [add your mission].

To maximize our effectiveness, we may seek to collaborate with other nonprofit organizations which qualify as nonprofit corporations under section 501(c) (3).

Personal Liability

No officer or director of this corporation shall be personally liable for the debts or obligations of the Corporation of any nature whatsoever, nor shall any of the property or assets of the officers or directors be subject to the payment of the debts or obligations of this corporation.

Dissolution

Upon the dissolution of the Corporation, assets shall be distributed for one or more exempt purposes within the meaning of Section 501(c) (3) of the Internal Revenue Code, or corresponding section of any future federal tax code, or shall be distributed to the federal government, or to a state or local government, for a public purpose. Any such assets not so disposed of shall be disposed of by a Court of Competent Jurisdiction of the county in which the principal office of the Corporation is then located, exclusively for such purposes or to such organization or organizations as said Court shall determine which are organized and operated exclusively for such purposes.

Prohibited Distributions

No part of the net earnings, or properties of this corporation, on dissolution or otherwise, shall inure to the benefit of, or be distributable to, its members, directors, officers or other private person or individual, except that the Corporation shall be authorized and empowered to pay reasonable compensation for services rendered and to make payments and distributions in furtherance of the tax- exempt purposes of the Corporation.

Restricted Activities

No substantial part of the Corporation's activities shall be the carrying on of propaganda, or otherwise attempting to influence legislation, and the Corporation shall not participate in, or intervene (including the publishing or distribution of statements) in any political campaign on behalf of or in opposition to any candidate for public office.

Prohibited Activities

Notwithstanding any other provision of these Articles, the Corporation shall not carry on any activities not permitted to be carried on (a) by a corporation exempt from federal income tax as an organization described by Section 501(c)(3) of the Internal Revenue Code, or the corresponding section of any future federal tax code, or (b) by a corporation, contributions to which are deductible under Section 170(c)(2) of the Internal Revenue Code, or the corresponding section of any future federal tax code.

Governance

The Corporation shall be governed by its board of directors.

Initial Directors

The initial directors of the Corporation shall be [Add board members' names].

Membership

The Corporation shall not have members; the management of the affairs of the Corporation shall be vested in a board of directors, as defined in the Corporation's bylaws.

Amendments

Any amendment to the Articles of Incorporation may be adopted by approval of two-thirds (2/3) of the board of directors.

2. MAIL IN YOUR OWN ARTICLES OF INCORPORATION

Here is a template of state and IRS-compliant Articles of Incorporation prepared by an attorney I paid $300 an hour. If you do not want to type this document, you can get it at *www.doyourownnonprofit.org*

[ENTER CORPORATION NAME]
ARTICLES OF INCORPORATION – NONPROFIT

The undersigned incorporator is an individual 18 years of age or older and adopts the following articles of incorporation to form a nonprofit corporation (Chapter 317A).

ARTICLE I
NAME AND ORGANIZATION

The legal name of this corporation shall be [Enter name of nonprofit].

ARTICLE II
DURATION

The period of duration of the Corporation shall be perpetual.

ARTICLE III
PURPOSE

The Corporation is a non-profit corporation organized exclusively for charitable, religious, educational, and scientific purposes, including, for such purposes, the making of distributions to organizations that qualify as exempt organizations, under Section 501 (c)(3) of the Internal Revenue Code, or the corresponding section of any future federal tax code.

The mission of the Corporation is to [Enter mission].

To maximize our effectiveness, we may seek to collaborate with other non-profit organizations which qualify as non-profit corporations under section 501(c) (3).

ARTICLE IV
NON-PROFIT NATURE / BENEFITS

4.01 Non-profit Nature

The Corporation is not organized and shall not be operated for the private gain of any person. The property of the Corporation is irrevocably dedicated to its charitable, religious, educational or scientific purposes. No part of the assets, receipts, or net earnings of the Corporation shall inure to the benefit of, or be distributed to, any individual. The Corporation may, however, pay reasonable compensation for services rendered, and make other payments and distributions consistent with these Articles.

4.02 Personal Liability

No officer or director of this corporation shall be personally liable for the debts or obligations of the Corporation of any nature whatsoever, nor shall any of the property or assets of the officers or directors be subject to the payment of the debts or obligations of this corporation.

4.03 Dissolution

Upon the dissolution of the corporation, assets shall be distributed for one or more exempt purposes within the meaning of Section 501(c)(3) of the Internal Revenue Code, or corresponding section of any future federal tax code, or shall be distributed to the federal government, or to a state or local government, for a public purpose. Any such assets not so disposed of shall be disposed of by a Court of Competent Jurisdiction of the county in which the principal office of the corporation is then located, exclusively for such purposes or to such organization or organizations as said Court shall determine which are organized and operated exclusively for such purposes.

4.04 Restricted Activities

No substantial part of the Corporation's activities shall be the carrying on of propaganda, or otherwise attempting to influence legislation, and the Corporation shall not participate in, or intervene (including the publishing or distribution of statements) in any political campaign on behalf of or in opposition to any candidate for public office.

4.05 Prohibited Activities

Notwithstanding any other provision of these Articles, the Corporation shall not carry on any activities not permitted to be carried on (a) by a corporation exempt from federal income tax as an organization described by Section 501(c)(3) of the Internal Revenue Code, or the corresponding section of any future federal tax code, or (b) by a corporation, contributions to which are deductible under Section 170(c)(2) of the Internal Revenue Code, or the corresponding section of any future federal tax code.

ARTICLE V
BOARD OF DIRECTORS

The Corporation shall be governed by its board of directors as defined in the Corporation's bylaws.

ARTICLE VI
MEMBERSHIP

The Corporation shall have no members.

ARTICLE VII
AMENDMENTS

Any amendment to the Articles of Incorporation may be adopted by approval of two-thirds (2/3) of the board of directors.

ARTICLE VIII
ADDRESSES OF THE CORPORATION

The physical address of the Corporation is:

The principal mailing address of the Corporation is:

ARTICLE IX
APPOINTMENT OF REGISTERED AGENT

The registered agent of the Corporation and address shall be [Enter Registered Agent name and address, must be a street address, not a postal box].

ARTICLE X
INCORPORATOR

The incorporator of the Corporation is [Enter incorporator name and address].

Certificate of Adoption of Articles of Incorporation

In witness whereof, I, the undersigned, have hereunto subscribed my name for the purpose of forming the corporation under the laws of the State of Minnesota and certify I have executed these Articles of Incorporation this _____ day of _____, 20__.

Incorporator Name _____
Address, City, State, ZIP _____
Incorporator Signature _____
Phone Number _____

The incorporator can also be the registered agent and can also be one of the board members.

Sign the Articles of Incorporation and mail with $70 check or money order for regular processing, or $90 for expedited processing. Make check payable to *MN Secretary of State*.

Mail to:

> Minnesota Secretary of State - Business Services
> Retirement Systems of Minnesota Building
> 60 Empire Drive, Suite 100
> St Paul, MN 55103
>
> Phone Lines (9 a.m. - 4 p.m., M-F):
> Metro Area 651-296-2803
> Greater MN 1-877-551-6767

ANNUAL RENEWAL

Annual renewal is due by December 31 each year. There is no filing fee.

Annual renewals can be filed online at *http://mblsportal.sos.state.mn.us/Business/Search*. Login and then scroll down under Business to *Renewal*.

If you prefer, you can file the paper renewal located at *http://www.sos.state.mn.us/media/1534/nonprofitrenewal.pdf*

CHARITABLE REGISTRATION EXEMPTION

Charitable registration is not the same as incorporation or annual renewal. The Secretary of State handles the incorporation and renewal process. The Attorney General (AG) handles the granting of permission to raise funds in Minnesota. The AG is the watch dog for fraud and scams.

If your organization has less than $25,000 revenues in a year, conducts all its activities and fundraising with unpaid volunteers (no paid staff or independent contractors), and does not hire professional solicitors, you do not have to file for charitable registration.

CHARITABLE REGISTRATION – INITIAL FILING

If you do not meet the exemption requirements, you must file a charitable registration application before you can raise funds in Minnesota. The filing fee is $25. The penalty for raising funds without registering is $25,000 for each occurrence.

Here is where you get the form to file: https://www.ag.state.mn.us/Charity/Forms/Char_InitRegForm.pdf

Follow the instructions, complete the form (not unusual for page 5 to be all zeros on the initial registration), and assemble the requested documents.

There are two choices for filing:

1. Email to *charity.registration@ag.state.mn.us* and make payment online at *http://www.ag.state.mn.us/Charity/CharFees.aspx*
2. Mail in the registration with $25 check to:

    Minnesota Attorney General's Office
    Charities Division
    445 Minnesota Street, Suite 1200
    St. Paul, MN 55101-2130

More information is available at *www.ag.state.mn.us/charity*
Phone numbers: (651) 296-3353 or (800) 657-3787

CHARITABLE REGISTRATION – ANNUAL REPORT

Your annual report is due by the 15th day of the seventh month after the end of the fiscal year. If your organizations fiscal year ends December 31, your Charitable Registration Annual Report is due by July 15. Minnesota gives a four-month extension if you apply before the due date for the annual report. If you don't file or request an extension, there is a $50 late fee.

Visit *www.ag.state.mn.us/Charity/ExtensionRequest.aspx* to request an extension.

There are two choices for filing:

1. Email to *charity.registration@ag.state.mn.us* and make payment online at *http://www.ag.state.mn.us/Charity/CharFees.aspx*
2. Mail in the registration with $25 check to:

    Minnesota Attorney General's Office
    Charities Division
    445 Minnesota Street, Suite 1200
    St. Paul, MN 55101-2130

More information is available at www.ag.state.mn.us/charity
Phone numbers: (651) 296-3353 or (800) 657-3787

SALES TAX EXEMPTION

Once you have your approval letter from IRS for 501(c)(3) tax-exempt status, you can apply for Sales Tax Exemption which allows you to purchase for the organization without paying sales tax. It does not relieve you from collecting sales tax for items sold by the organization.

To apply, fill out Minnesota Form ST16, *Application for Nonprofit Exempt Status—Sales Tax*. You can do an internet search for the form or go to *http://www.revenue.state.mn.us/Forms_and_Instructions/st16.pdf*

Send the completed application along with all required documentation to:

Minnesota Revenue
Mail Station 6330
St. Paul, MN 55146-6330

If you have questions, call Minnesota Revenue at 651-296-6181 or 800-657-3777.

CHAPTER 11

LET'S CREATE BYLAWS

"A goal is a dream with a deadline."
—Napoleon Hill

STANDARD OPERATING PROCEDURES

Have you ever been around someone who was or is in the military? They have a language all their own. One of the things they often say is, "It's SOP." What they mean is that it is *standard operating procedure*. In my ten years in the United States Air Force, there were SOPs for everything, normally in the form of regulations, manuals, and technical orders. There was written guidance that addressed just about every foreseeable event or circumstance.

If you look at the nonprofit you are creating as its own army to do good things in the world then you will see the need for SOPs to make your operation as efficient as an Army or Marine rifle platoon. Because you are the incorporator, you may be filling the shoes right now of the Platoon Leader (President), Platoon Sergeant (Vice President), Company Clerk (Secretary), or Quartermaster (Treasurer). People have to know the rules and what is expected so that they can follow them. Your nonprofit corporation bylaws establish the rules or SOPs in which business is conducted.

CREATING THE CONSTITUTION

Another way to understand the significance of bylaws is to think of them as the organization's constitution. You cannot put everything in the Constitution, only the really important stuff. Once written and approved, it's the way things are done. If you ever want to change something, you have to amend the bylaws, just as you would have to amend the Constitution. Keep trivial aspects that are subject to change (such as the day of the week board meetings are held) out of the bylaws. Be sure to attach any changes to the bylaws directly to the master copy as soon as changes are made.

It is common to make a change, put it in the meeting minutes, but then forget which meeting the change was made, and never attach the change to the master copy of the bylaws. The solution is to assign the responsibility to update the bylaws to one of the board positions. If you keep it simple, there will not be many changes to keep up with.

BYLAW CONTENTS

So exactly what do you put in the bylaws? It depends on which state you live in, but there are some general items addressed in virtually all nonprofit bylaws:

- Name of the organization and the mission.
- How many board members (minimum established by the state) and what constitutes a quorum? (Normally a majority of members need to be present.)
- Qualifications of board members.
- How officers and board members will be elected and how long they will serve. If you want them to be able to serve more than one term, you need to say so in the bylaws. Also, address limitations on personal liability and the procedures for removing a board member if necessary.
- Duties of Board Members.

- Procedures for calling and conducting meetings, including special and emergency board meetings; and when regular meetings will be held (suggest monthly, bi-monthly, or quarterly, nothing more specific so that you have the flexibility to make changes). In this era of electronics, will you allow board meetings by email, teleconferencing, and/or electronic conferencing venues such as Skype? All states allow meetings to take place using technology as long as everyone can hear everyone else, and each can communicate with the rest of the board members.
- How will conflicts of interest be handled? I suggest you reference a conflict of interest policy so that if you ever change procedures, you can more easily update a conflict of interest policy than making formal changes to bylaws.
- How funds will be accounted for and disbursed.
- If the nonprofit has members, what are the classes and rights of membership? (Most 501(c)(3) nonprofits do not have members).
- How committees can be convened and dissolved.
- How can bylaws be changed (for example, by majority vote of the board)?
- Accounting or fiscal year that fits the normal flow of activities. Education-related activities might need a different fiscal year than an animal shelter. December 31 is the most common fiscal year end.
- Authorize bank signatories.

The following pages include a template for nonprofit bylaws drawn up by an attorney so that you know it contains legal integrity and everything you need to be compliant with the state and IRS. You can delete or modify anything that does not apply to your organization or anything you would rather do differently, but you might be hard pressed to find anything to add. The attorney who created this document was very thorough.

> THE ATTORNEY WHO CREATED THIS DOCUMENT WAS VERY THOROUGH.

Here are a few things to be aware of in this template:

- 2.03 Nonprofit Status and Exempt Activities Limitation. This section says that you are already approved for 501(c)(3) status. I have it from the attorney's lips that "It is standard practice" to include this clause now so that you do not have to amend the Bylaws later (per Steve Eggleston, J.D.).
- 4.01 Number of Directors. The template is set up with a minimum of 5 directors to cover the four main positions of President, Vice President, Secretary, and Treasurer, and one extra for a tie breaker. You can change to another number to fit your board as long as you have the minimum.
- 4.08 Manner of Acting. Paragraph (d) allows meetings to take place by means of modern technology, so everyone does not have to be physically present to be considered in attendance. The entire meeting can be by telephone!
- 5.3 Informal Action by The Board of Directors. This section gives the Board the right to give consent without a meeting, allowing email to be used when a meeting is not needed.
- 8.02 Fiscal Year. The fiscal year is January 1 – December 31. You can change the date if your organization needs a different fiscal year.
- 8.04 Nondiscrimination. You may change the nondiscrimination section, but I suggest you leave race, age, gender, and physical disability.
- 11.03 Means and Conditions of Disclosure. Nonprofits have a lawful obligation to disclose certain documents. This section should be reviewed to make sure that the procedure for disclosure (using the organization's website) is the way you want to handle disclosure. It is the easiest and eliminates all individual inquiries to see your documents, and thus reduces administrative workload. You decide and change the wording to suit your organization.

This template is available at www.doyourownnonprofit.org

[NAME OF CORPORATION]
NONPROFIT CORPORATE BYLAWS

ARTICLE I
NAME

1.01 Name

The name of this corporation shall be [insert the legal name of your nonprofit].

[Example: The name of this corporation shall be Transcontinental Humanitarian Corp.]

ARTICLE II
PURPOSES AND POWERS

2.01 Purpose

[Insert the legal name of your nonprofit] – hereafter referred to as "The Corporation" is a nonprofit corporation and shall be operated exclusively for charitable, religious, educational, and scientific purposes, including, for such purposes, the making of distributions to organizations that qualify as exempt organizations, under Section 501 (c) (3) of the Internal Revenue Code, or the corresponding section of any future federal tax code.

The Corporation's purpose is to [insert description of specific purpose].

[Example: The Corporation's purpose is to address, educate, coordinate, and provide aid and relief to eradicate chronic malnutrition and hunger on a local and global level.]

To maximize our impact on current efforts, we may seek to collaborate with other nonprofit organizations which fall under the 501(c) (3) section of the Internal Revenue Code and are operated exclusively for charitable, religious, educational and scientific purposes.

2.02 Powers

The Corporation shall have the power, directly or indirectly, alone or in conjunction or cooperation with others, to do any and all lawful acts which may be necessary or convenient to affect the charitable purposes, for which The Corporation is organized, and to aid or assist other organizations or persons whose activities further accomplish, foster, or attain such purposes. The powers of The Corporation may include, but not be limited to, the acceptance of contributions from the public and private sectors, whether financial or in-kind contributions.

2.03 Nonprofit Status and Exempt Activities Limitation.

Nonprofit Legal Status. The Corporation is a nonprofit corporation, recognized as tax-exempt under Section 501(c) (3) of the United States Internal Revenue Code.

Exempt Activities Limitation. Notwithstanding any other provision of these Bylaws, no Director, officer, employee, member, or representative of this corporation shall take any action or carry on any activity by or on behalf of The Corporation not permitted to be taken or carried on by an organization exempt under Section 501(c) (3) of the Internal Revenue Code as it now exists or may be amended, or by any organization contributions to which are deductible under

Section 170(c) (2) of such Code and Regulations as it now exists or may be amended. No part of the net earnings of The Corporation shall inure to the benefit or be distributable to any Director, officer, member, or other private person, except that The Corporation shall be authorized and empowered to pay reasonable compensation for services rendered and to make payments and distributions in furtherance of the purposes set forth in the Articles of Incorporation and these Bylaws.

Distribution Upon Dissolution. Upon termination or dissolution of The Corporation, any assets lawfully available for distribution shall be distributed to one (1) or more qualifying organizations described in Section 501(c) (3) of the Internal Revenue Code (or described in any corresponding provision of any successor statute) which organization or organizations have a charitable purpose which, at least generally, includes a purpose similar to the terminating or dissolving corporation.

The organization to receive the assets of The Corporation hereunder shall be selected at the discretion of a majority of the managing body of The Corporation, and if its members cannot so agree, then the recipient organization shall be selected pursuant to a Verified Petition in equity, or such other court of appropriate jurisdiction, filed in a court of proper jurisdiction against The Corporation, by one (1) or more of its managing body, which Verified Petition shall contain such statements as reasonably indicate the applicability of this section. The court upon a finding that this section is applicable shall select the qualifying organization or organizations to receive the assets to be distributed, giving preference if practicable to organizations located within the state.

In the event that the court shall find that this section is applicable but that there is no qualifying organization known to it which has a charitable purpose, which, at least generally, includes a purpose similar to The Corporation, then the court shall direct the distribution of its assets lawfully available for distribution to the Treasurer of the State to be added to the general fund.

ARTICLE III
MEMBERSHIP

3.01 No Membership Classes

The Corporation shall have no members who have any right to vote or title or interest in or to The Corporation, its properties, and franchises.

3.02 Non-Voting Affiliates

The Board of Directors may approve classes of non-voting affiliates with rights, privileges, and obligations established by the Board. Affiliates may be individuals, businesses, and other organizations that seek to support the mission of The Corporation. The Board, a designated committee of the Board, or any duly-elected officer in accordance with Board policy, shall have authority to admit any individual or organization as an affiliate, to recognize representatives of affiliates, and to make determinations as to affiliates' rights, privileges, and obligations. At no time shall affiliate information be shared with or sold to other organizations or groups without the affiliate's consent. At the discretion of the Board of Directors, affiliates may be given endorsement, recognition and media coverage at fundraising activities, clinics, other events or at The Corporation website. Affiliates have no voting rights and are not members of The Corporation.

> THE BOARD OF DIRECTORS MAY APPROVE CLASSES OF NON-VOTING AFFILIATES WITH RIGHTS, PRIVILEGES, AND OBLIGATIONS ESTABLISHED BY THE BOARD.

3.03 Dues

Any dues for affiliates shall be determined by the Board of Directors.

ARTICLE IV
BOARD OF DIRECTORS

4.01 Number of Directors

The Corporation shall have a Board of Directors consisting of at least 5 and no more than 15 Directors. Within these limits, the Board may increase or decrease the number of Directors serving on the Board, including for the purpose of staggering the terms of Directors.

4.02 Powers

All corporate powers shall be exercised by or under the authority of the Board and the affairs of The Corporation shall be managed under the direction of the Board, except as otherwise provided by law.

4.03 Terms

a. All Directors shall be elected to serve a two-year term; however, the term may be extended until a successor has been elected.
b. Director terms shall be staggered so that approximately half the number of Directors will end their terms in any given year.
c. Directors may serve terms in succession.
d. The term of office shall be considered to begin the first month of the fiscal year, and end the last day of the second fiscal year in office, unless the term is extended until such time as a successor has been elected.

4.04 Qualifications and Election of Directors

In order to be eligible to serve as a Director on the Board of Directors, the individual must be 18 years of age. Directors may be elected at any Board meeting by the majority vote of the existing Board of Directors. The election of Directors to replace those who have fulfilled their term of office shall take place during the first month of each new fiscal year.

4.05 Vacancies

The Board of Directors may fill vacancies due to the expiration of a Director's term of office, resignation, death, or removal of a Director or may appoint new Directors to fill a previously unfilled Board position, subject to the maximum number of Directors under these Bylaws.

Unexpected Vacancies. Vacancies in the Board of Directors due to resignation, death, or removal shall be filled by the Board for the balance of the term of the Director being replaced.

4.06 Removal of Directors

A Director may be removed by [insert your choice of "a majority or "two-thirds" or "three-fourths"] vote of the Board of Directors then in office, if:

a. the Director is absent and unexcused from two or more meetings of the Board of Directors in a twelve-month period. The Board President is empowered to excuse Directors from attendance for a reason deemed adequate by the Board President. The President shall not have the power to excuse him/herself from the Board meeting attendance, and in that case, the Board Vice President shall excuse the President. Or:
b. for cause or no cause, if before any meeting of the Board at which a vote on removal will be made, the Director in question is given electronic or written notification of the Board's intention to discuss her/his case and is given the opportunity to be heard at a meeting of the Board.

4.07 Board of Directors Meetings

Regular Meetings. The Board of Directors shall have a minimum of four (4) regular meetings each calendar year at times and places fixed by the Board. Board meetings shall be held upon four (4) days' notice by first-class mail, electronic mail, or facsimile transmission or forty-eight (48) hours' notice delivered personally or by telephone. If sent by mail, facsimile transmission, or electronic mail, the notice shall be deemed to be delivered upon its deposit in the mail or transmission system. Notice of meetings shall specify the place, day, and hour of meeting. The purpose of the meeting need not be specified.

Special Meetings. Special meetings of the Board may be called by the President, Vice President, Secretary, Treasurer, or any two (2) other Directors of the Board of Directors. A special meeting must be preceded by at least 2-days' notice to each Director of the date, time, and place, but not the purpose, of the meeting.

Waiver of Notice. Any Director may waive notice of any meeting.

4.08 Manner of Acting.

Quorum. A majority of the Directors in office immediately before a meeting shall constitute a quorum for the transaction of business at that meeting of the Board. No business shall be considered by the Board at any meeting at which a quorum is not present.

Majority Vote. Except as otherwise required by law or by the Articles of Incorporation, the act of the majority of the Directors present at a meeting at which a quorum is present shall be the act of the Board.

Hung Board Decisions. On the occasion that Directors of the Board are unable to make a decision based on a tied number of votes, the President or Treasurer in the order of presence shall have the power to swing the vote based on his/her discretion.

Participation. Except as required otherwise by law, the Articles of Incorporation, or these Bylaws, Directors may participate in a regular or special meeting through the use of any means of communication by which all Directors participating may simultaneously hear each other during the meeting, including in person, internet video meeting or by telephonic conference call.

4.09 Compensation for Board Service

Directors shall receive no compensation for carrying out their duties as Directors. The Board may adopt policies providing for reasonable reimbursement of Directors for expenses incurred in conjunction with carrying out Board responsibilities, such as travel expenses to attend Board meetings.

4.10 Compensation for Professional Services by Directors

Directors are not restricted from being remunerated for professional services provided to The Corporation. Such remuneration shall be reasonable and fair to The Corporation and must be reviewed and approved in accordance with the Board Conflict of Interest Policy and applicable state law.

ARTICLE V
COMMITTEES

5.01 Committees

The Board of Directors may, by the resolution adopted by a majority of the Directors then in office, designate one or more committees, each consisting of two or more Directors, to serve at the pleasure of the Board. Any committee, to the extent provided in the resolution of the Board, shall have all the authority of the Board, except that no committee, regardless of Board resolution, may:

a. take any final action on matters which also requires Board members' approval or approval of a majority of all members;
b. fill vacancies on the Board of Directors or in any committee which has the authority of the Board;
c. amend or repeal Bylaws or adopt new Bylaws;

d. amend or repeal any resolution of the Board of Directors which by its express terms is not so amendable or repealable;
e. appoint any other committees of the Board of Directors or the members of these committees;
f. expend corporate funds to support a nominee for Director; or
g. approve any transaction
   i. to which The Corporation is a party and one or more Directors have a material financial interest; or
   ii. between The Corporation and one or more of its Directors or between The Corporation or any person in which one or more of its Directors have a material financial interest.

5.02 Meetings and Action of Committees

Meetings and action of the committees shall be governed by, and held and taken in accordance with, the provisions of Article IV of these Bylaws concerning meetings of the Directors, with such changes in the context of those Bylaws as are necessary to substitute the committee and its members for the Board of Directors and its members, except that the time for regular meetings of committees may be determined either by resolution of the Board of Directors or by resolution of the committee. Special meetings of the committee may also be called by resolution of the Board of Directors. Notice of special meetings of committees shall also be given to any and all alternate members, who shall have the right to attend all meetings of the committee. Minutes shall be kept of each meeting of any committee and shall be filed with the corporate records. The Board of Directors may adopt rules for the governing of the committee not inconsistent with the provision of these Bylaws.

5.03 Informal Action by The Board of Directors

Any action required or permitted to be taken by the Board of Directors at a meeting may be taken without a meeting if consent in writing, setting forth the action so taken, shall be agreed by the consensus of a quorum. For purposes of this section, an email transmission from an email address on record constitutes a valid writing. The intent of this provision is to allow the Board of Directors to use email to approve actions, as long as a quorum of Board members gives consent.

ARTICLE VI
OFFICERS

6.01 Board Officers

The officers of The Corporation shall be a Board President, Vice President, Secretary, and Treasurer, all of whom shall be chosen by, and serve at the pleasure of, the Board of Directors. Each Board officer shall have the authority and shall perform the duties set forth in these Bylaws or by resolution of the Board or by direction of an officer authorized by the Board to prescribe the duties and authority of other officers. The Board may also appoint additional Vice Presidents and such other officers as it deems expedient for the proper conduct of the business of The Corporation, each of whom shall have such authority and shall perform such duties as the Board of Directors may determine. No Board officer may act in more than one capacity where action of two or more officers is required.

6.02 Term of Office

Each officer shall serve a two-year term of office and may serve consecutive terms of office.

6.03 Removal and Resignation

The Board of Directors may remove an officer at any time, with or without cause. Any officer may resign at any time by giving written notice to The Corporation without prejudice to the rights, if any, of The Corporation under any contract to which the officer is a party. Any resignation shall take effect at the date of the receipt of the notice or at any later time specified in the notice unless otherwise specified in the notice. The acceptance of the resignation shall not be necessary to make it effective.

6.04 Board President

The Board President shall be the Chief Volunteer Officer of The Corporation. The Board President shall lead the Board of Directors in performing its duties and responsibilities, including, if present, presiding at all meetings of the Board of Directors, and shall perform all other duties incident to the office or properly required by the Board of Directors.

6.05 Vice President

In the absence or disability of the Board President, the ranking Vice President or Vice President designated by the Board of Directors shall perform the duties of the Board President. When so acting, the Vice President shall have all the powers of and be subject to all the restrictions upon the Board President. The Vice President shall have such other powers and perform such other duties prescribed for them by the Board of Directors or the Board President.

6.06 Secretary

The Secretary shall keep or cause to be kept a book of minutes of all meetings and actions of Directors and committees of Directors. The minutes of each meeting shall state the time and place that it was held and such other information as shall be necessary to determine the actions taken and whether the meeting was held in accordance with the law and these Bylaws. The Secretary shall cause notice to be given of all meetings of Directors and committees as required by the Bylaws. The Secretary shall have such other powers and perform such other duties as may be prescribed by the Board of Directors or the Board President. The Secretary may appoint, with approval of the Board, a Director to assist in performance of all or part of the duties of the Secretary.

6.07 Treasurer

The Treasurer shall be the lead Director for oversight of the financial condition and affairs of The Corporation. The Treasurer shall oversee and keep the Board informed of the financial condition of The Corporation and of audit or financial review results. In conjunction with other Directors or officers, the Treasurer shall oversee budget preparation and shall ensure that appropriate financial reports, including an account of major transactions and the financial condition of The Corporation, are made available to the Board of Directors on a timely basis or as may be required by the Board of Directors. The Treasurer shall perform all duties properly required by the Board of Directors or the Board President. The Treasurer may appoint, with approval of the Board, a qualified fiscal agent or member of the staff to assist in performance of all or part of the duties of the Treasurer.

6.08 Non-Director Officers

The Board of Directors may designate additional officer positions of The Corporation and may appoint and assign duties to other non-Director officers of The Corporation.

ARTICLE VII
CONTRACTS, CHECKS, LOANS, INDEMNIFICATION AND RELATED MATTERS

7.01 Contracts and Other Writings

Except as otherwise provided by resolution of the Board or Board policy, all contracts, deeds, leases, mortgages, grants, and other agreements of The Corporation shall be executed on its behalf by the Treasurer or other persons to whom The Corporation has delegated authority to execute such documents in accordance with policies approved by the Board.

7.02 Checks, Drafts

All checks, drafts, or other orders for payment of money, notes, or other evidence of indebtedness issued in the name of The Corporation, shall be signed by such officer or officers, agent or agents, of The Corporation and in such manner as shall from time to time be determined by resolution of the Board.

7.03 Deposits

All funds of The Corporation not otherwise employed shall be deposited from time to time to the credit of The Corporation in such banks, trust companies, or other depository as the Board or a designated committee of the Board may select.

7.04 Loans

No loans shall be contracted on behalf of The Corporation, and no evidence of indebtedness shall be issued in its name unless authorized by resolution of the Board. Such authority may be general or confined to specific instances.

7.05 Indemnification

Mandatory Indemnification. The Corporation shall indemnify a Director or former Director, who was wholly successful, on the merits or otherwise, in the defense of any proceeding to which he or she was a party because he or she is or was a Director of The Corporation against reasonable expenses incurred by him or her in connection with the proceedings.

Permissible Indemnification. The Corporation shall indemnify a Director or former Director made a party to a proceeding because he or she is or was a Director of The Corporation, against liability incurred in the proceeding, if the determination to indemnify him or her has been made in the manner prescribed by the law and payment has been authorized in the manner prescribed by law.

Advance for Expenses. Expenses incurred in defending a civil or criminal action, suit or proceeding may be paid by The Corporation in advance of the final disposition of such action, suit or proceeding, as authorized by the Board of Directors in the specific case, upon receipt of (i) a written affirmation from the Director, officer, employee or agent of his or her good faith belief that he or she is entitled to indemnification as authorized in this Article, and (ii) an undertaking by or on behalf of the Director, officer, employee or agent to repay such amount, unless it shall ultimately be determined that he or she is entitled to be indemnified by The Corporation in these Bylaws.

Indemnification of Officers, Agents, and Employees. An officer of The Corporation who is not a Director is entitled to mandatory indemnification under this Article to the same extent as a Director. The Corporation may also indemnify and advance expenses to an employee or agent of The Corporation who is not a Director, consistent with the law of the state in which the nonprofit is incorporated and public policy, provided that such indemnification, and the scope of such indemnification, is set forth by the general or specific action of the Board or by contract.

ARTICLE VIII
MISCELLANEOUS

8.01 Books and Records

The Corporation shall keep correct and complete books and records of account and shall keep minutes of the proceedings of all meetings of its Board of Directors, a record of all actions taken by Board of Directors without a meeting, and a record of all actions taken by committees of the Board. In addition, The Corporation shall keep a copy of The Corporation's Articles of Incorporation and Bylaws as amended to date.

8.02 Fiscal Year

The fiscal year of The Corporation shall be from January 1 to December 31 of each year.

8.03 Conflict of Interest

The Board shall adopt and periodically review a Conflict of Interest Policy to protect The Corporation's interest when it is contemplating any transaction or arrangement which may benefit any Director, officer, employee, affiliate, or member of a committee with Board-delegated powers.

8.04 Nondiscrimination Policy

The officers, Directors, committee members, employees, and persons served by this corporation shall be selected entirely on a nondiscriminatory basis with respect to age, sex, race, religion, and national origin. It is the policy of The Corporation not to discriminate on the basis of race, creed, ancestry, marital status, gender, age, physical disability, veteran's status, political service or affiliation, color, religion, or national origin.

8.05 Bylaw Amendment

These Bylaws may be amended, altered, repealed, or restated by a vote of the majority of the Board of Directors then in office at a meeting of the Board, provided, however,

- a. that no amendment shall be made to these Bylaws which would cause The Corporation to cease to qualify as an exempt corporation under Section 501 (c) (3) of the Internal Revenue Code, or the corresponding section of any future Federal tax code; and,
- b. that an amendment does not affect the voting rights of Directors. An amendment that does affect the voting rights of Directors

further requires ratification by [choose between "a majority" or "a two-thirds"] vote of a quorum of Directors at a Board meeting.
c. that all amendments be consistent with the Articles of Incorporation.

ARTICLE IX
COUNTERTERRORISM AND DUE DILIGENCE POLICY

In furtherance of its exemption by contributions to other organizations, domestic or foreign, The Corporation shall stipulate how the funds will be used and shall require the recipient to provide The Corporation with detailed records and financial proof of how the funds were utilized.

Although adherence and compliance with the U.S. Department of the Treasury's publication entitled the "Voluntary Best Practice for U.S.-Based Charities," is not mandatory, The Corporation willfully and voluntarily recognizes and puts to practice these guidelines and suggestions to reduce, develop, re-evaluate and strengthen a risk-based approach to guard against the threat of diversion of charitable funds or exploitation of charitable activity by terrorist organizations and their support networks.

The Corporation shall also comply and put into practice the federal guidelines, suggestions, laws and limitations set forth by pre-existing U.S. legal requirements related to combating terrorist financing, which include, but are not limited to, various sanctions programs administered by the Office of Foreign Assets Control (OFAC) in regard to its foreign activities.

> THE CORPORATION SHALL STIPULATE HOW THE FUNDS WILL BE USED AND SHALL REQUIRE THE RECIPIENT TO PROVIDE THE CORPORATION WITH DETAILED RECORDS AND FINANCIAL PROOF OF HOW THE FUNDS WERE UTILIZED.

ARTICLE X
DOCUMENT RETENTION POLICY

10.01 Purpose

The purpose of this Document Retention Policy is to establish standards for document integrity, retention, and destruction, and to promote the proper treatment of The Corporation's records.

10.02 Policy

Section 1. General Guidelines. Records should not be kept if they are no longer needed for the operation of the business or required by law. Unnecessary records should be eliminated from the files. The cost of maintaining records is an expense which can grow unreasonably if good housekeeping is not performed. A mass of records also makes it more difficult to find pertinent records. [Optional: "Where possible, the nonprofit shall adopt a digital, non-paper filing and retention system.]

From time to time, The Corporation may establish retention or destruction policies or schedules for specific categories of records in order to ensure legal compliance, and also to accomplish other objectives, such as preserving intellectual property and cost management. Several categories of documents that warrant special consideration are identified below. While minimum retention periods are established, the retention of the documents identified below and of documents not included in the identified categories should be determined primarily by the application of the general guidelines affecting document retention, as well as the exception for litigation relevant documents and any other pertinent factors.

Section 2. Exception for Litigation Relevant Documents. The Corporation expects all officers, Directors, and employees to comply fully with any published records retention or destruction policies and schedules, provided that all officers, Directors, and employees should note the following general exception to any stated destruction schedule: If you believe, or The Corporation informs you, that corporate records are relevant to litigation, or potential litigation (i.e., a dispute that could result in litigation), then you must preserve those records until it is determined that the records are no longer needed. That exception supersedes any previously or subsequently established destruction schedule for those records.

> THE CORPORATION EXPECTS ALL OFFICERS, DIRECTORS, AND EMPLOYEES TO COMPLY FULLY WITH ANY PUBLISHED RECORDS RETENTION OR DESTRUCTION POLICIES AND SCHEDULES.

Section 3. Minimum Retention Periods for Specific Categories

a. Corporate Documents. Corporate records include The Corporation's Articles of Incorporation, Bylaws and IRS Application for Exemption. Corporate records should be retained permanently. IRS regulations require that the Form 1023 be available for public inspection upon request.
b. Tax Records. Tax records include, but may not be limited to, documents concerning payroll, expenses, proof of contributions made by donors, accounting procedures, and other documents concerning The Corporation's revenues. Tax records should be retained for at least seven (7) years from the date of filing the applicable return.
c. Employment Records/Personnel Records. State and federal statutes require The Corporation to keep certain recruitment, employment, and personnel information. The Corporation should also keep personnel files that reflect performance reviews and any complaints brought against The Corporation or

individual employees under applicable state and federal statutes. The Corporation should also keep in the employee's personnel file all final memoranda and correspondence reflecting performance reviews and actions taken by or against personnel. Employment applications should be retained for three (3) years. Retirement and pension records should be kept permanently. Other employment and personnel records should be retained for seven years.

d. Board and Board Committee Materials. Meeting minutes should be retained in perpetuity in The Corporation's minute book. A clean copy of all other Board and Board Committee materials should be kept for no less than three (3) years by The Corporation.

e. Press Releases/Public Filings. The Corporation should retain permanent copies of all press releases and publicly filed documents under the theory that The Corporation should have its own copy to test the accuracy of any document a member of the public can theoretically produce against The Corporation.

f. Legal Files. Legal counsel should be consulted to determine the retention period of particular documents, but legal documents should generally be maintained for a period of ten (10) years.

g. Marketing and Sales Documents. The Corporation should keep final copies of marketing and sales documents for the same period of time it keeps other corporate files, generally three (3) years. An exception to the three-year policy may be sales invoices, contracts, leases, licenses, and other legal documentation. These documents should be kept for at least three (3) years beyond the life of the agreement.

h. Development/Intellectual Property and Trade Secrets. Development documents are often subject to intellectual property protection in their final form (e.g., patents, trademarks, service marks, and copyrights). The documents detailing the development process are often also of value to The Corporation and are protected as a trade secret where The Corporation:

    i. derives independent economic value from the secrecy of the information; and

    ii. has taken affirmative steps to keep the information confidential.

The Corporation should keep all documents designated as containing trade secret information for at least the life of the trade secret.

i. Contracts. Final, execution copies of all contracts entered into by The Corporation should be retained. The Corporation should retain copies of the final contracts for at least three (3) years beyond the life of the agreement, and longer in the case of publicly filed contracts.
j. Correspondence. Unless correspondence falls under another category listed elsewhere in this policy, correspondence should generally be saved for two (2) years.
k. Banking and Accounting. Accounts payable ledgers and schedules should be kept for seven (7) years. Bank reconciliations, bank statements, deposit slips and checks (unless for important payments and purchases) should be kept for three (3) years. Any inventories of products, materials, and supplies and any invoices should be kept for seven (7) years.
l. Insurance. Expired insurance policies, insurance records, accident reports, claims, etc. should be kept permanently.
m. Audit Records. External audit reports should be kept permanently. Internal audit reports should be kept for three (3) years.

Section 4. Electronic Mail. E-mail that needs to be saved should be either:

i. printed in hard copy and kept in the appropriate file; or
ii. downloaded to a computer file and kept electronically or on disk as a separate file. The retention period depends upon the subject matter of the e-mail, as covered elsewhere in this policy.

ARTICLE XI
Transparency and Accountability
Disclosure of Financial Information
With The General Public

11.01 Purpose

By making full and accurate information about its mission, activities, finances, and governance publicly available, The Corporation practices and encourages transparency and accountability to the general public. This Policy will:

a. indicate which documents and materials produced by The Corporation are presumptively open to staff and/or the public,
b. indicate which documents and materials produced by The Corporation are presumptively closed to staff and/or the public, and
c. specify the procedures whereby the open/closed status of documents and materials can be altered.

The details of this Policy are as follows:

11.02 Financial and IRS documents (Form 1023 and the Form 990). The Corporation shall provide its Internal Revenue Forms 990, 990-T, 1023 and 5227, Bylaws, Conflict of Interest Policy, and financial statements to the general public for inspection free of charge.

11.03 Means and Conditions of Disclosure

The Corporation shall make "Widely Available" the aforementioned documents on its internet website to be viewed and inspected by the general public when possible and practical to do so.

a. When made available electronically, the documents shall be posted in a format that allows an individual using the Internet to

access, download, view and print them in a manner that exactly reproduces the image of the original document filed with the IRS (except information exempt from public disclosure requirements, such as contributor lists).
b. The website shall clearly inform readers that the document is available and provide instructions for downloading it.
c. The Corporation shall not charge a fee for downloading the information. Documents shall not be posted in a format that would require special computer hardware or software (other than software readily available to the public free of charge).
d. The Corporation shall inform anyone requesting the information where this information can be found, including the web address. This information must be provided immediately for in-person requests and within seven (7) days for mailed requests.

11.04 IRS Annual Information Returns (Form 990 series)

The Corporation shall submit the appropriate Form 990 series return to its Board of Directors prior to the filing of Form 990. While neither the approval of Form 990 or a review of the Form 990 is required under federal law, The Corporation's Form 990 shall be submitted to each member of the Board of Director's via hard copy or email at least ten (10) days before Form 990 is filed with the IRS.

11.05 Board

a. All Board deliberations shall be open to the public except where the Board passes a motion to make any specific portion confidential.
b. All Board minutes shall be open to the public once accepted by the Board, except where the Board passes a motion to make any specific portion confidential.
c. All papers and materials considered by the Board shall be open to the public following the meeting at which they are considered, except where the Board passes a motion to make any specific paper or material confidential.

11.06 Staff Records

a. All staff records shall be available for consultation by the staff member concerned or by their legal representatives.
b. No staff records shall be made available to any person outside The Corporation except the authorized governmental agencies.
c. Within The Corporation, staff records shall be made available only to those persons with managerial or personnel responsibilities for that staff member, except that
d. Staff records shall be made available to the Board when requested.

11.07 Donor Records

a. All donor records shall be available for consultation by the members and donors concerned or by their legal representatives.
b. No donor records shall be made available to any other person outside The Corporation except the authorized governmental agencies.
c. Within The Corporation, donor records shall be made available only to those persons with managerial or personnel responsibilities for dealing with those donors, except that donor records shall be made available to the Board when requested.

ARTICLE XII
CODE OF ETHICS AND WHISTLEBLOWER POLICY

12.01 Purpose

The Corporation requires and encourages Directors, officers and employees to observe and practice high standards of business and personal ethics in the conduct of their duties and responsibilities. The employees and representatives of The Corporation must practice honesty and integrity in fulfilling their responsibilities and comply with all applicable laws and regulations. It is the intent of The Corporation to adhere to all laws and regulations that apply to The Corporation, and the underlying purpose of this policy is to support The Corporation's goal of legal compliance. The support of all corporate staff is necessary to achieving compliance with various laws and regulations.

12.02 Reporting Violations

If any Director, officer, staff or employee reasonably believes that some policy, practice, or activity of The Corporation is in violation of law, a written complaint must be filed by that person with the Vice President or the Board President.

12.03 Acting in Good Faith

Anyone filing a complaint concerning a violation or suspected violation of a law or regulation must be acting in good faith and have reasonable grounds for believing the information disclosed indicates a violation. Any allegations that prove not to be substantiated and which prove to have been made maliciously or knowingly to be false shall be viewed as a serious disciplinary offense.

12.04 Retaliation

A person filing the aforesaid complaint is protected from retaliation only if she/he brings the alleged unlawful activity, policy, or practice to the attention of The Corporation and provides The Corporation with a reasonable opportunity to investigate and correct the alleged unlawful activity. The protection described below is only available to individuals that comply with this requirement.

The Corporation shall not retaliate against any Director, officer, staff or employee who in good faith, has made a protest or raised a complaint against some practice of The Corporation or of another individual or entity with whom The Corporation has a business relationship, on the basis of a reasonable belief that the practice is in violation of law or a clear mandate of public policy.

The Corporation shall not retaliate against any Director, officer, staff or employee who discloses or threatens to disclose to a supervisor or a public body, any activity, policy, or practice of The Corporation that the individual reasonably believes is in violation of a law or a rule, or regulation mandated pursuant to law or is in violation of a clear mandate of public policy concerning the health, safety, welfare, or protection of the environment.

12.05 Confidentiality

Violations or suspected violations may be submitted on a confidential basis by the complainant or may be submitted anonymously. Reports of violations or suspected violations shall be kept confidential to the extent possible, consistent with the need to conduct an adequate investigation.

12.06 Handling of Reported Violations

The Board President or Vice President shall notify the sender and acknowledge receipt of the reported violation or suspected violation within five business days. All reports shall be promptly investigated by the Board and its appointed committee, and appropriate corrective action shall be taken if warranted by the investigation.

This policy shall be made available to all Directors, officers, staffs or employees and they shall have the opportunity to ask questions about the policy.

ARTICLE XIII
AMENDMENT OF ARTICLES OF INCORPORATION

13.01 Amendment

Any amendment to the Articles of Incorporation may be adopted by approval of two-thirds (2/3) of the Board of Directors.

CERTIFICATE OF ADOPTION OF BYLAWS

I do hereby certify that the above stated Bylaws of The Corporation were approved by The Corporation's Board of Directors on _____ and constitute a complete copy of the Bylaws of The Corporation.

Secretary _____
Date: _____

CHAPTER 12

DEVELOP A CONFLICT OF INTEREST POLICY

"Opportunities don't happen; you create them."
—CHRIS GROSSER

SET PERSONAL INTERESTS ASIDE

IRS is concerned about conflicts of interest within 501(c) (3) corporations. A conflict of interest occurs when someone in a responsible position within a nonprofit has competing interests and is faced with making choices that could benefit themselves (or friends and family members) to the detriment of the organization. Board members and directors of a nonprofit have a first duty to promote the best interests of the organization. They must lay their personal interests aside when

> A CONFLICT OF INTEREST OCCURS WHEN SOMEONE IN A RESPONSIBLE POSITION WITHIN A NONPROFIT HAS COMPETING INTERESTS AND IS FACED WITH MAKING CHOICES THAT COULD BENEFIT THEMSELVES.

conducting the business of the nonprofit. Should a conflict of interest arise, it should be disclosed immediately.

Below is a sample Conflict of Interest Policy from IRS containing the minimum requirements. In addition, IRS wants board members and directors to fill out an annual Conflict of Interest Statement which should be kept on file with the corporation's other important documents. If you do not want to type out the sample Conflict of Interest Policy or develop a Conflict of Interest Annual Statement, free templates come with the Nonprofit Template Package Deal on my website at *www.doyourownnonprofit.com* Proceeds go to *Pasture Valley Children Missions.*

IRS SAMPLE CONFLICT OF INTEREST POLICY

CONFLICT OF INTEREST POLICY
[NAME OF ORGANIZATION]

Adopted on: _____

ARTICLE I
PURPOSE

The purpose of the conflict of interest policy is to protect [NAME OF ORGANIZATION] (the "Organization") interest when it is contemplating entering into a transaction or arrangement that might benefit the private interest of an officer or director of the Organization or might result in a possible excess benefit transaction. This policy is intended to supplement but not replace any applicable state and federal laws governing conflict of interest applicable to nonprofit and charitable organizations.

ARTICLE II
DEFINITIONS

1. Interested Person

Any director, principal officer, or member of a committee with governing board delegated powers, who has a direct or indirect financial interest, as defined below, is an interested person.

2. Financial Interest

A person has a financial interest if the person has, directly or indirectly, through business, investment, or family:

a. An ownership or investment interest in any entity with which the Organization has a transaction or arrangement,
b. A compensation arrangement with the Organization or with any entity or individual with which the Organization has a transaction or arrangement, or
c. A potential ownership or investment interest in, or compensation arrangement with, any entity or individual with which the Organization is negotiating a transaction or arrangement.

Compensation includes direct and indirect remuneration as well as gifts or favors that are not insubstantial.

A financial interest is not necessarily a conflict of interest. Under Article III, Section 2, a person who has a financial interest may have a conflict of interest only if the appropriate governing board or committee decides that a conflict of interest exists.

ARTICLE III
PROCEDURES

1. Duty to Disclose

In connection with any actual or possible conflict of interest, an interested person must disclose the existence of the financial interest and be given the opportunity to disclose all material facts to the directors and members of committees with governing board delegated powers considering the proposed transaction or arrangement.

2. Determining Whether a Conflict of Interest Exists

After disclosure of the financial interest and all material facts, and after any discussion with the interested person, s/he shall leave the governing board or committee meeting while the determination of a conflict of interest is discussed and voted upon. The remaining board or committee members shall decide if a conflict of interest exists.

3. Procedures for Addressing the Conflict of Interest

a. An interested person may make a presentation at the governing board or committee meeting, but after the presentation, s/he shall leave the meeting during the discussion of, and the vote on, the transaction or arrangement involving the possible conflict of interest.
b. The chairperson of the governing board or committee shall, if appropriate, appoint a disinterested person or committee to investigate alternatives to the proposed transaction or arrangement.
c. After exercising due diligence, the governing board or committee shall determine whether the Organization can obtain with reasonable efforts a more advantageous transaction or arrangement from a person or entity that would not give rise to a conflict of interest.
d. If a more advantageous transaction or arrangement is not reasonably possible under circumstances not producing a conflict of interest, the governing board or committee shall determine by a majority vote of the

disinterested directors whether the transaction or arrangement is in the Organization's best interest, for its own benefit, and whether it is fair and reasonable. In conformity with the above determination, it shall make its decision as to whether to enter into the transaction or arrangement.

4. Violations of the Conflicts of Interest Policy

a. If the governing board or committee has reasonable cause to believe a member has failed to disclose actual or possible conflicts of interest, it shall inform the member of the basis for such belief and afford the member an opportunity to explain the alleged failure to disclose.
b. If, after hearing the member's response and after making further investigation as warranted by the circumstances, the governing board or committee determines the member has failed to disclose an actual or possible conflict of interest, it shall take appropriate disciplinary and corrective action.

ARTICLE IV
RECORDS OF PROCEEDINGS

The minutes of the governing board and all committees with board delegated powers shall contain:

a. The names of the persons who disclosed or otherwise were found to have a financial interest in connection with an actual or possible conflict of interest, the nature of the financial interest, any action taken to determine whether a conflict of interest was present, and the governing board or committee's decision as to whether a conflict of interest in fact existed.
b. The names of the persons who were present for discussions and votes relating to the transaction or arrangement, the content of the discussion, including any alternatives to the proposed transaction or arrangement, and a record of any votes taken in connection with the proceedings.

ARTICLE V
COMPENSATION

a. A voting member of the governing board who receives compensation, directly or indirectly, from the Organization for services is precluded from voting on matters pertaining to that member's compensation.
b. A voting member of any committee whose jurisdiction includes compensation matters and who receives compensation, directly or indirectly, from the Organization for services is precluded from voting on matters pertaining to that member's compensation.
c. No voting member of the governing board or any committee whose jurisdiction includes compensation matters and who receives compensation, directly or indirectly, from the Organization, either individually or collectively, is prohibited from providing information to any committee regarding compensation.

ARTICLE VI
ANNUAL STATEMENTS

Each director, principal officer and member of a committee with governing board delegated powers shall annually sign a statement which affirms such person:

a. Has received a copy of the conflict of interest policy,
b. Has read and understands the policy,
c. Has agreed to comply with the policy, and
d. Understands the Organization is charitable and in order to maintain its federal tax exemption, it must engage primarily in activities which accomplish one or more of its tax-exempt purposes.

ARTICLE VII
REVIEWS

To ensure the Organization operates in a manner consistent with charitable purposes and does not engage in activities that could jeopardize its tax-exempt status, periodic reviews shall be conducted. The periodic reviews shall, at a minimum, include the following subjects:

a. Whether compensation arrangements and benefits are reasonable, based on competent survey information, and the result of arm's length bargaining,
b. Whether partnerships, joint ventures, and arrangements with management organizations conform to the Organization's written policies, are properly recorded, reflect reasonable investment or payments for goods and services, further charitable purposes and do not result in inurement, impermissible private benefit or in an excess benefit transaction.

ARTICLE VIII
USE OF OUTSIDE EXPERTS

When conducting the periodic reviews as provided for in Article VII, the Organization may, but need not, use outside advisors. If outside experts are used, their use shall not relieve the governing board of its responsibility for ensuring periodic reviews are conducted.

In addition to the Conflict of Interest Policy, you need to create a Conflict of Interest Annual Statement for board members (and managers and employees if desired) to sign. One might look something like this 2-page document:

PERSONAL AND CONFIDENTIAL
[NAME OF ORGANIZATION]

Conflict of Interest Statement

1. As a(n) _____ of this Organization, I acknowledge that I:

    a. Received a copy of the Organization's Conflict of Interest Policy dated _____ _____, 20_____.
    b. Read and understood the policy;
    c. Agree to comply with the spirit and intent of the policy and will disclose any potential conflicts, other than those stated on next page, as they may arise before completion of my next conflict of interest statement; and
    d. Understand that the Organization is a charitable organization, and in order to maintain its federal tax exemption, it must engage primarily in activities which accomplish one or more of its tax-exempt purposes.

2. Based on a review of the Organization's Conflict of Interest Policy, are you aware of any interest that you or a related person may have that could give rise to a conflict of interest? If yes, please complete Attachment A to this form.

    _____Yes   _____No

My answers above are accurately stated to the best of my knowledge and belief.

Dated   _____
Signature   _____
Printed Name _____

DR. KITTY BICKFORD, DBS, CPC

PERSONAL AND CONFIDENTIAL
[NAME OF ORGANIZATION]

Conflict of Interest Statement

Attachment A

1. Please list all relationships (if any) between you or a "related party" (as defined below) with the Organization that involve an actual or potential financial benefit to you or the related party or that otherwise may represent a conflict of interest within the spirit and intent of the policy. Include an estimate of the related actual or potential financial benefit.

2. Please list any business dealings during the past year (or, as applicable, since your last submission of this Conflict of Interest Statement) of which you are aware in which you or a "related party" (as defined below) have received a salary, gifts, or loans from any source from which the Organization obtains goods or services or otherwise has business dealings:

_____

_____

_____

_____

_____

3. Please list any potential or pending transaction to which the Organization is a party and in which you or a "related party" (as defined below) has a direct or indirect interest.

_____

_____

_____

_____

_____

NOTE: A "related party" (as defined in this policy) is a family member; a business or organization of which the person signing this statement or a family member owns or expects to own, directly or indirectly, more than a 5% interest; has a beneficial interest in a trust that owns directly or indirectly more than a 5% interest; or is a director, officer, or employee. A "family member" is a parent (or more remote ancestor), spouse, brother, sister, spouse of a brother or sister, child, step-child, grandchild, great-grandchild or spouse of a child, step-child, or great-grandchild of the person signing this statement.

CHAPTER 13

HOLD AND DOCUMENT THE FIRST BOARD MEETING

"You miss 100% of the shots you don't take."
—WAYNE GRETZKY

Did you know that IRS and auditors consider board meeting minutes as legal documents that will hold up in court? Many legal minds believe that if it is not in the meeting minutes, it did not occur because the meeting minutes are formal records of the business conducted and the decisions made by an organization.

There is no set format for meeting minutes, and each organization should decide how the meeting minutes should look. When secretaries of the board change, the format often changes to suit the new secretary. As long as the required information is recorded, the format is not critical. Copies of meeting minutes from previous meetings should be given to board members for review and approval. All meeting minutes should be filed in a safe, accessible place.

There are some things that should be included in every set of meeting minutes:

1. Name of the organization
2. Date and time of the meeting
3. Who ran the meeting
4. Who was there and who was absent
5. What was voted on and whether anyone abstained from voting
6. All motions made
7. When the meeting ended
8. Who prepared the meeting minutes

Personal opinions and heated arguments or discussions should not be included. Minutes should cover the business of the organization, not document disagreements among members. Do not include in-depth details of reports, better to just attach the reports to the minutes.

If you are about to conduct your first board meeting, you want to include the business of setting up the organization and getting it running. Your meeting minutes should include the following:

1. Initial board members and the offices, if any, that they hold (for example president, vice president, secretary, treasurer, or board member)
2. How you will elect or appoint board members in the future
3. Approve application for an FEIN number (if not already done)
4. Approve development of Articles of Incorporation (if not already done)
5. Adopt the organization's bylaws
6. Approve applying for 501(c)(3) status with IRS
7. Approve setting up banking accounts and decide how funds will be handled, and who is authorized to conduct banking activities
8. Approve the Conflict of Interest Policy
9. Determine fiscal accounting year

Your board meeting minutes and any resolutions about banking passed at board meetings may be needed to open a bank account. Many banks need proof of who is allowed to sign checks and conduct the banking business for the organization. Your board meeting minutes show who is in which office and can list who is allowed to do banking business. I included an Initial Organizational Meeting Minutes template as part of the package deal under the state templates tab at *www.doyourownnonprofit.org* if you don't want to create your own from scratch.

PART II
IRS FORM 1023 APPLICATION FOR TAX-EXEMPT STATUS

CHAPTER 14

REQUEST FOR RECOGNITION OF EXEMPTION

"Whether you think you can or think you can't, you're right."
—Henry Ford

WHERE TO BEGIN

If you have completed all the requirements in previous chapters, you are ready to complete the federal application, and you have two choices of which form to use based on mission, where you operate in the world, and projected budget. Your choices are:

- IRS Form 1023, *Application for Recognition of Exemption under Section 501(c) (3) of the Internal Revenue Code* (available at *www.irs.gov*)
- IRS Form 1023-EZ, *Streamlined Application for Recognition of Exemption Under Section 501(c) (3) of the Internal Revenue Code* (available online only at *www.pay.gov*)

Make sure you use the newest Form 1023 available because IRS will return the application unprocessed if you use an old form. The current form at the time of printing is dated December 2017.

Information on the Form 1023-EZ is in Part IV of this book. The rest of Part II and all of Part III deal with Form 1023, *Application for Recognition of Exemption under Section 501(c) (3) of the Internal Revenue Code* and required schedules.

WHAT TO EXPECT

Once you mail your application package to IRS, you will get a letter about a month after you file that confirms IRS got your package and will process it one of two ways: fast or slow. They do not tell you which one! You get a form letter that everyone gets, and there is no reason to stress over whether they will assign an agent. Even if they do, it is only to ask some questions.

Wait about three months after that initial letter for IRS to send you a *determination letter*. It is called a determination letter because the first sentence says, "We are pleased to tell you that we have *determined* you're exempt from federal income tax under Internal Revenue Code (IRC) Section 501(c) (3)." The wording changes from time to time, but the meaning is the same. The determination letter is a form letter that looks very much like the FEIN confirmation letter.

IRS says it takes 6 – 12 months to process your application, but if you use the instructions in this book, you should hear back in 3 – 4 months. As long as you file within 27 months of getting approved by the state, your 501(c) (3) status will be effective the date the state approved your nonprofit status. IRS backdates it so that there is no gap in 501(c) (3) coverage. If you file after 27 months from the date of incorporation with the state, IRS does not backdate the application and approves it with a current effective date.

Guard the determination letter with your life; IRS will not replace it unless you fill out Form 4506-A and wait up to 60 days for a replacement copy. The determination letter is your proof you have 501(c) (3) tax-exempt status and is required for grants. It is a public record that anyone can ask to see or have a copy. You are obligated by IRS regulations to give anyone who asks copies of your federal application for 501(c)(3) tax-exempt status, your annual information tax returns, and your determination letter from IRS. It is a condition of getting tax-exempt 501(c)(3) status. You are allowed to charge a reasonable fee for copies and postage if applicable.

IMPORTANT!

If you do not hear from IRS within about 60 days from the time they send the letter acknowledging they got your package, call them at 877-829-5500. I have had dozens of cases in which IRS agents said they sent follow-up questionnaires or determination letters that never arrived. In the case of a questionnaire, IRS gives you a deadline to answer. If you don't get the notice, you don't answer it. In that case, IRS takes your money, cancels your application and says, "Oh well…" Check on it if you don't hear back in 60 days or so after the form letter that says they got your package. It is a precaution to avoid IRS bureaucracy and unnecessary additional costs. Best to call early in the day. By afternoon, you normally get a recording that says, "due to high call volumes, your call will not go through, please call another day."

If your application contains everything IRS needs to know, a determination letter will be issued. If not, you will receive requests for additional clarification or information. Needing more information can delay approval, but not the effective date. If you apply within 27 months, it will be the day the state approved your incorporation no matter when IRS gets around to approving your application.

You can get expedited handling if you request it for a compelling reason. To ask for expedited handling, send a letter with the package requesting priority approval and give a good, compelling reason. Good, compelling reasons include:

- pending grants that will not be made without 501(c)(3) status;
- your organization is created to provide relief to victims of disasters such as recent floods, hurricanes, tsunamis, or tornadoes;

- your application has been delayed because of problems at IRS due to no fault of your organization.

IRS estimates that it takes over 100 hours to complete the 501(c)(3) process. Hopefully, this book will cut down those hours by more than half, but grit your teeth, get ready to dig in, and describe your organization completely so that a quick determination can be made without required follow-up from IRS. If you put in the work upfront to do it right the first time, you will not have to deal with ongoing correspondence and paperwork from IRS.

DISCLOSURE

Did you know that you are allowed to see and have a copy of Form 1023 for most nonprofit organizations that have been approved after July 15, 1987? You can be charged a fair price for making copies. Not all organizations know they are required to disclose their applications, so you can ask for a copy of the paperwork and quote the IRS guidance located at *www.irs.gov* (search for Public Disclosure and Availability of Exempt Organizations Returns and Applications: Documents Subject to Public Disclosure) which states (last updated on April 21, 2017):

Public Disclosure and Availability of Exempt Organizations Returns and Applications: Documents Subject to Public Disclosure

What tax documents must an exempt organization make available for public inspection and copying?

An exempt organization must make available for public inspection its exemption application. An exemption application includes the Form 1023 (for organizations recognized as exempt under Internal Revenue Code section 501(c)(3)), Form 1024 (for organizations recognized as exempt under most other paragraphs of section 501(c)), or the letter submitted under the paragraphs for which no form is prescribed, together with supporting documents and any letter or document issued by the IRS concerning the application. A political organization exempt from taxation under section 527(a) must make available for public inspection and copying its notice of status, Form 8871.

In addition, an exempt organization must make available for public inspection and copying its annual return. Such returns include Form 990, Return of Organization Exempt From Income Tax, Form 990-EZ, Short Form Return of Organization Exempt From Income Tax, Form 990-PF, Return of Private Foundation, Form 990-BL, Information and Initial Excise Tax Return for Black Lung Benefit Trusts and Certain Related Persons, and the Form 1065, U.S. Partnership Return of Income.

A section 501(c)(3) organization must make available for public inspection and copying any Form 990-T, Exempt Organization Business Income Tax Return, filed after August 17, 2006. Returns must be available for a three-year period beginning with the due date of the return (including any extension of time for filing). For this purpose, the return includes any schedules, attachments, or supporting documents that relate to the imposition of tax on the unrelated business income of the charity. See Public Inspection and Disclosure of Form 990-T for more information.

An exempt organization is not required to disclose Schedule K-1 of Form 1065 or Schedule A of Form 990-BL. With the exception of private foundations, an exempt organization is not required to disclose the name and address of any contributor to the organization.

A political organization exempt from taxation under section 527(a) must make available for inspection and copying its report of contributions and expenditures on Form 8872, Political Organization Report of Contributions and Expenditures. However, such organization is not required to make available its return on Form 1120-POL, U.S. Income Tax Return for Certain Political Organizations.

Many organizations choose to meet the disclosure requirements by putting their public documents online.

If you contact an organization and they do not give you a copy of their paperwork, you can make a stink and report them. But why bother?

Instead, use a Form 4506-A and ask IRS for a copy. They take up to 60 days to send it, but you can get a copy. It is free up to 100 pages, and twenty cents a page over 100 pages. Fill out the form, check Form 1023 in Box 9 and either mail or fax it to:

> Internal Revenue Service
> Attn: Correspondence Unit
> P.O. Box 2508, Room 4024
> Cincinnati, OH 45201
> Fax No. (513) 263-3434

CHAPTER 15

PART I

IDENTIFICATION OF APPLICANT

"Setting a goal is not the main thing. It is deciding how you will go about achieving it and staying with that plan."

—Tom Landry

ONE STEP AT A TIME

You are now at the point where you will begin filling out the actual application. No need to be overwhelmed – simply take it one step at a time, and you will get through this.

NOTE: If you are unsure of what to put in any section of the Form 1023, call IRS Tax Exempt and Government Entities Customer Account Services at (877) 829-5500. Better to ask now than to delay the approval of your application for months.

Start by pulling up the online application at *http://www.irs.gov/pub/irs-pdf/f1023.pdf* or Google Form 1023. A good rule of thumb is to print the blank application and work on it in sections, then fill out the application online and print it. The form allows you to save your work (the first time), but if you need to change anything or finish later, the form does not allow for changes, so you have to start over. An alternative would be to save the form to your computer and complete it one page at a time by using the Adobe PDF function *Fill and Sign*. You can complete a page, save it, close out, open again, and go to the next page and repeat. Probably easier to fill out the entire form online and print it complete so that no changes are needed. I strongly suggest that you print a copy of all completed sections as you finish them online in case your computer malfunctions, or for some reason the online document does not save your answers the way it should. That way you will not have come up with the answers again. (Work smart – take all necessary precautions.)

Below I have listed what is needed for each specific line in the application:

Line 1: Full name of organization (exactly as it appears in your organizing document and FEIN)
Enter your organization's name from state incorporation document, including amendments. Be sure to include Inc. or Corp. if that is part of the organization's official name. Do not abbreviate or use acronyms, spell out the complete name as it is listed on the approved state incorporation.

Line 2: c/o Name
If you want a specific person to be the go-to person for correspondence, put in an *in-care-of* name here. If you are the founder and are using your personal address, you can use your name. You can also leave it blank.

Line 3: Mailing address
This will be the address you want correspondence sent to. A post office box is fine if that is where you get your mail. (For overseas addresses, list information in this order: city, province or state, and fully-spelled-out country, followed by the customary postal code for the country.)

Line 4: Employer Identification Number (EIN)
Enter the FEIN issued by IRS. It is 9-digits long: the first two digits, a dash, and the last 7 digits. For example, the EIN for Pasture Valley Children Missions (a nonprofit I founded) is 35-2468924. If you do not have an FEIN number, go back to Chapter 4 and follow the instructions. You can get a number online from IRS. IRS does not accept applications for organizations without FEIN numbers. If you cannot get the FEIN online, you can mail or fax IRS Form SS-4.

Line 5: Month the annual accounting period ends (01-12)
Your accounting year should end at a logical point. For example, a school organization may end on June 30 or July 31. Most other organizations have December 31 as the accounting period end. Put the month in which you plan to end your annual accounting period. The last day of the accounting period will be the last day of the month you select. Also, check your bylaws to verify the accounting period. Depending on the month you select, your first accounting period may be less than one calendar year. For example, if you start your nonprofit in May and your accounting year ends in December, you will only have a seven-month accounting period the first year. This is not a problem.

Line 6a: Primary contact
Who do you want IRS to talk with if they need to discuss your application, organizational documents, bylaws, or other such matters? This person can be an officer, director, or any other person you designate to discuss your organization's rules and procedures. It can also be you. Another option is to designate an authorized representative, attorney, or accountant to represent you by filing an IRS Form 2848 with your application.

Line 6b: Phone
What is the contact person's phone number? Include the area code.

Line 6c: Fax (optional)
Enter fax number if you have one.

Line 7
If you have authorized an attorney or accountant to talk with IRS on your behalf, check "Yes" and attach IRS Form 2848. If your contact is you or an officer on your board of directors, check "No."

Line 8
Is there anyone outside your organization that you have paid or promised to pay to:

- Help you fill out your Form 1023?
- Help you establish your organization?
- Set up fundraising programs?
- Handle tax matters?
- Prepare financials?
- Handle other organizational matters?

If you mark "Yes," you must provide the person's name, the name and address of the firm they represent, how much you paid or are going to pay, and exactly what the person has done or is doing. If not, then mark "No."

Line 9a: Organization's Website
If you have a website, list it here. The information you have on your actual website must match the information you include in this application. If you do not have a website, put in N/A. Also, if any other websites have your information on them or are maintained on your behalf, list them.

Line 9b: Email (optional)
If you want educational materials sent to you by IRS, give an email address if you have one. They will not contact you with confidential information by email but will use U.S. Postal Service, phone, or fax. If you do not have an official organization email address, you can use your personal email address. You do not have to include an email address.

Line 10

This item has to do with whether you will be required to file an annual information return using some version of Form 990. If you are a church, certain church affiliated organizations, or certain affiliates of government units, you are not required to file a Form 990. Include an explanation in the narrative section of why you think you do not need to file one of the versions of Form 990.

Private foundations must file a Form 990-PF regardless of gross receipts. For small budget organizations, you can do your information return online quickly. As long as you keep good records, it is not difficult to comply with the Form 990 requirement, especially if you set up your books using the same categories as are contained on Form 990. Many grant-making organizations check to see that you filed your Form 990 before they accept or approve your grant application.

> FOR SMALL BUDGET ORGANIZATIONS, YOU CAN DO YOUR INFORMATION RETURN ONLINE QUICKLY.

Failure to file a required Form 990 return for three years (in whatever version you must use) results in automatic revocation of 501(c)(3) status. When this occurs, you have 15 months to file your application all over again (and pay the fees again) to get your status back retroactive to the date of revocation. If you file after 15 months from being revoked, you lose tax-exempt status for the time you were revoked and the donations made to your organization during the time of revocation are not tax deductible to your donors.

Line 11

What approval or effective date is on your state incorporation? That is the date you use. If you choose to use an earlier date because you have been conducting business, you can request an earlier date. Just be aware that you must file for 501(c)(3) status within 27 months of beginning operations. Best to use the state approval date. If you do not know the date, you can contact the state Corporations Division. They will give you the date.

Line 12

Was your organization formed in another country outside the United States? Organizations formed in United States territories or possessions, Indian tribal or Alaska Native governments, or Washington, D.C. are considered domestic, not foreign. If you check "Yes," you must list the foreign country your organization was formed in. Otherwise, check "No."

Now that wasn't too painful, was it? In the next chapter, you'll fill out all the information needed regarding your organizational structure.

CHAPTER 16

PART II

ORGANIZATIONAL STRUCTURE

"Success is no accident. It is hard work, perseverance, learning, studying, sacrifice and most of all, love of what you are doing or learning to do."

—Pele

This section of the application has to do with your organizational structure. Your organization must be a corporation, one specific type of Limited Liability Corporation (LLC), or a trust in order to be eligible for 501(c) (3) status. In this section, you must select your form of organization and attach your organizing documents to the application.

Line 1: Corporation
IRS defines a corporation as:

> *"an entity organized under a Federal or state statute, or a statute of a federally recognized Indian tribal or Alaskan native government."*

Corporation is the most popular and frequent organizational structure for 501(c) (3) status. You get corporate status by filing Articles of Incorporation with the state (see Chapters 9 and 10). The state approves your paperwork and assigns the date you became a corporate entity. You must include an exact copy of your filed document with the Form 1023, as well as any amendments to the original document. If you do not have an exact copy, you can contact the state Corporations Division for another copy.

> CORPORATION IS THE MOST POPULAR AND FREQUENT ORGANIZATIONAL STRUCTURE FOR 501(C) (3) STATUS.

Line 2: Limited Liability Corporation

Not all Limited Liability Corporations or Companies are eligible for 501(c) (3) status. To qualify, all the members of an LLC must be other 501(c) (3) organizations. LLCs made up of individuals are not eligible for tax-exempt status. LLCs are owned by members; nonprofit organizations are not owned, they are separate entities. This structure of LLC organization is confusing, contradictory, and brings problems you may not want to try to solve. If you are contemplating LLC structure, contact an attorney for further guidance to avoid laborious paperwork with IRS and extended timeframe for approval (or outright rejection of your application).

Line 3: Unincorporated Association

An unincorporated association must have a written agreement laying out the purpose of the association. There must be at least two members. According to IRS instructions, "the articles of organization of an unincorporated association must include the name of your organization, your purpose, the date the document was adopted, and the signatures of at least two individuals." Date of adoption is important to IRS.

Line 4a: Trust

A trust can be established by a will or by a trust agreement or declaration of trust. If created by a will, a copy of the death certificate and a copy of pertinent parts of the will must be attached to the application. A trust involves three groups of people:

- The donor(s)
- The trustee(s)
- The beneficiaries

Trustees can be sued on behalf of the trust. Not all trust instruments and structures are eligible for 501(c)(3) status.

Line 4b: Have You Been Funded?

For a trust to exist and be legal, it must be funded with money or real or personal property.

Line 5: Bylaws

If you have bylaws, attach them. IRS does not require them, but if you do not have them, some of their questions about how you function as an organization will not be answered. In that case, they may not approve your application without further information. This could delay your application for many months. Be safe, send the bylaws and eliminate the delay.

CHAPTER 17

PART III

PROVISIONS IN YOUR ORGANIZING DOCUMENTS

"The difference between a successful person and others is not a lack of strength, not a lack of knowledge, but rather a lack of will."

—VINCE LOMBARDI

Line 1: Location of Purpose Clause

Your organizing document must contain a purpose clause that is consistent with IRS requirements. This question wants to know exactly where it is located in your Articles of Incorporation or Association, or Declaration of Trust. Here is the example of an acceptable purpose clause contained in the IRS instructions for completing Form 1023:

> *Said Corporation is organized exclusively for charitable, religious, educational, and scientific purposes, including, for such purposes, the making of distributions to organizations that qualify as exempt organizations under Section 501(c) (3) of the Internal Revenue Code, or the corresponding section of any future federal tax code.*

Find that statement in your Articles and put the page, article, and paragraph in the blank on line, (and on the checklist at the back of the application on page 28, item 1 of the Form 1023 application). Don't forget to check the box to the right showing you have the required clause in your organizing document.

Line 2a: Dissolution Clause
To be approved for nonprofit status by IRS, you must have a dissolution clause that states that if you stop being a tax-exempt organization, all your assets will be given to another nonprofit organization. Here is an example of an acceptable dissolution clause (some IRS agents have accepted the first sentence only, but many agents look for the whole thing):

> *Upon the dissolution of the corporation, assets shall be distributed for one or more exempt purposes within the meaning of Section 501(c) (3) of the Internal Revenue Code, or corresponding section of any future federal tax code, or shall be distributed to the federal government, or to a state or local government, for a public purpose. Any such assets not so disposed of shall be disposed of by a Court of Competent Jurisdiction of the county in which the principal office of the corporation is then located, exclusively for such purposes or to such organization or organizations as said Court shall determine which are organized and operated exclusively for such purposes.*

Don't forget to check the box to the right showing you have the required clause in your organizing document.

Line 2b: Location of Dissolution Clause
From your organizing document, list the page, article, and paragraph of the dissolution clause. Then go to page 28 of the Form 1023 application and include the same information in the checklist where indicated.

Line 2c: Operation of State Law
If you checked 2a, you do not check this box. Most people will not use this block of the application. If you use this block, remember to check the box and fill in the state.

CHAPTER 18

PART IV

NARRATIVE DESCRIPTION OF YOUR ACTIVITIES

"If you can't explain it simply, you don't understand it well enough."
—Albert Einstein

THE HEART OF THE APPLICATION

You have come to the heart of your application, and it is now time to touch the heart of the IRS agent who will process your package. This is your chance, in a few pages, to describe the mission you are undertaking to do good things in the world. The key to getting your application approved lies in your willingness to put forth the effort to make your vision come alive. You have to answer the questions in the IRS agent's mind; not just the ones on the application, but the other ones that any interested person would want to know when finding out about your mission.

What do you tell people about your organization when you are explaining it one-on-one or in a small group? How did your organization come into existence? What was the deciding impetus that led to its creation? What excites you most about it? Who is involved? What are their qualifications? What do you want to accomplish? How are you going to accomplish it? How will you pay for it (make sure this information agrees with your financial section of the application)? How will you select the people, groups, or organizations you will help?

Remember to answer the questions asked on the application in enough detail to answer the *Who, What, When, Where, How, How Much,* and *Why* of each question.

NO RIGHT OR WRONG WAY

There is no right or wrong way format the narrative section, but by definition, a narrative can be an essay, biographical sketch, or autobiography (in this case for the organization), usually in chronological or other logical order. Use positive, powerful terms and word choices. Don't limit your future growth, but at the same time, do not take on the world. For example, do not say you are going to provide laptop computers to three rural schools in Alabama. Later you may want to provide iPads or work with schools in Mississippi as well. Instead, you might say you are going to improve technology access to rural schools in the southern United States, beginning with providing laptop computers to three rural schools in Alabama. In the narrative, you can show a small start, and give your organization room to grow so that you don't have to go back later and ask IRS to approve expanding your mission. Make it big now and grow into it later.

> THERE IS NO RIGHT OR WRONG WAY FORMAT THE NARRATIVE SECTION.

DR. KITTY BICKFORD, DBS, CPC

TELL YOUR STORY

Tell a story with your narrative and weave in the important points as part of the story. Be careful in this section not to refer to the organization with ownership; it is a separate entity that is not owned by anyone. Another way to get your mission across is to add copies of brochures, flyers, handouts, printed copies of website pages, and any other written material that will expand the IRS agent's understanding of what you are trying to do. You will also want to add short biographies of the board of directors demonstrating how they are qualified to perform the organization's mission, and attach a resume or curriculum vitae for each board member to the application package. Why? Because if you don't, sometimes IRS comes back and asks for a resume showing at least three years employment and address information. Best to put it in the first time and avoid any potential delay in processing.

You might also want to justify your procedures and structure by citing IRS regulations. You can quote specific content in the instruction booklet for filling out Form 1023, recite guidance given on the IRS website for nonprofit organizations, and quote or mention passages of IRS Revenue Rulings found at *http://www.irs.gov/Charities-&-Nonprofits/Archive-of-Published-Guidance*. An example of a Revenue Ruling you might use for tax deductibility of donated items would be Revenue Ruling 2002-67, which can be reviewed at *http://www.irs.gov/pub/irs-drop/rr-02-67.pdf* It states that:

> "A donor may use an established used car pricing guide to determine the fair market value of a single donated car if the guide lists a sales price for a car that is the same make, model, and year, sold in the same area, and in the same condition, as the donated car. However, a donor may not use an established used car pricing guide to determine the fair market value of a single donated car if the guide does not list a sales price for a car in the same condition as the donated car. In such a case, the donor must use some other method that is reasonable under the circumstances to determine the value of the car. See Publication 561, "Determining the Value of Donated Property."

Your narrative might read: "Donated property to this organization will be accounted for using Publication 561 and the intent of Revenue Ruling 2002-67 which held that a donor must use reasonable methods to determine the value of the donated property."

By inserting periodic Revenue Rulings and IRS published guidance into your narrative, you give credibility to your application package and show the IRS agent that you are abreast of guidelines that affect your nonprofit operation.

NOTE: Every page of your application and all attachments must have the organization name and EIN on it. If you are typing your narrative, you may want to include this information in a header.

CHAPTER 19

PART V

COMPENSATION AND OTHER FINANCIAL ARRANGEMENTS

"How wonderful it is that no one need wait a single moment before starting to improve the world."

—ANNE FRANK

POSSIBLE CONFLICTS OF INTEREST

This section of your application is designed to disclose any conflicts of interest, personal profit to organization officials (or their friends, business associates, or family members), and undue influence because of relationships, contracts, and mingled loyalties between organizations. If you are a new organization with beginning operations, this section will be easy and fast to complete because chances are you that will not have any of these issues to disclose.

Line 1a: List Name, Title, Mailing Address, and Compensation for All Officers, Directors, And Trustees

Normally board members are not compensated, but can be reimbursed for out-of-pocket expenses necessary to perform their tasks on behalf of the nonprofit. Reimbursements are NOT compensation and are not reported in this section.

For the addresses requested in this question, you can use the organization's mailing address if desired. Include exact compensation if possible. Compensation includes salary or other compensation, deferred retirement, health insurance coverage paid for by the organization, value of vehicles provided, and any other compensation in kind for use of equipment or personal items provided including travel or memberships.

If no compensation is given, enter *None*. Information given in this section must match the financial data given in Part IX. Compensation must be reasonable for the position. Compensation paid to employees that is in any way linked to income or donations to the organization (such as percentages paid based on fundraising) waves a big red flag at IRS.

Line 1b: Five Highest Compensated Employees Over $50,000 A Year That Are Not Listed In Line 1a

If you have anyone who fits this category, provide total compensation information. If not, put *None* and move on. This information must match Part IX. Compensation must be reasonable for the position.

Line 1c: Five Highest Compensated Independent Contractors Over $50,000 a Year

IRS Publication 15 gives a general rule for independent contractors, which is:

> *"that an individual is an independent contractor if you, the person for whom the services are performed, have the right to control or direct only the result of the work and not the means and methods of accomplishing the result."*

If you do not have anyone in that category, put *None* and move on. This information must match Part IX, Financial Data.

Line 2a: Family or Business Relationships
Here is a make-or-break question on your Form 1023. If there are a husband and wife on the board or members that are related by blood or business, take caution. The IRS is going to look hard at your organization to make sure that related parties do not make up over half the voting power of the organization. It's best to have either husband or wife or to add board members so that the related parties do not have the majority of the vote. If none, check "No." If there are relationships, check "Yes."

Explain the relationship in the narrative section by answering any questions about the relationship that a reasonable person would have while eliminating the concern on the part of the IRS agent that abuse may occur as a result of this relationship. If it is a husband and wife on the board, make sure there are more board members who are not related so that no family has more than 49% of the voting power on the board. An explanation of husband and wife relationship might read:

> IT'S BEST TO HAVE EITHER HUSBAND OR WIFE OR TO ADD BOARD MEMBERS SO THAT THE RELATED PARTIES DO NOT HAVE THE MAJORITY OF THE VOTE.

John and Sally Smith are happily married and are anxious to work together to accomplish the mission of this organization.

IRS instructions list the following family relationships that need to be disclosed:

- Spouses
- Ancestors
- Children
- Grandchildren
- Great grandchildren
- Siblings (whole or half-blood)
- Spouses for any of these

Line 2b: Business Relationships with Officers, Directors, Or Trustees
Another make-or-break question on Form 1023. Other than being a part of the organization as an officer, director, or trustee, does *the organization* have any business relationship with these members? For example, do you hire one of the board members to perform any services for the organization? If so, this must be disclosed. If none, check "No." Working together at the same company that has no dealings with the nonprofit is not a relationship that requires disclosure. IRS is looking for conflicts of interest. Working together at the same place is not a conflict of interest. You can still both be on the board.

If there are relationships, check "Yes." Explain them in the narrative section answering any questions about the relationship that a reasonable person would have and eliminating the concern on the part of the IRS agent that abuse may occur as a result of this relationship.

Line 2c: Relationships Between Board Members and Highest Compensated Employees Or Independent Contractors
You guessed it – this is yet another make-or-break question. If there are any relationships between officers, directors, or trustees, and your five highest compensated employees or contractors who receive over $50,000 per year, you need to disclose it here. Explain it in the narrative section answering any questions about the relationship that a reasonable person would have and eliminating the concern on the part of the IRS agent that abuse may occur as a result of this relationship.

Line 3a: Name, Qualifications, Average Hours Worked and Duties for Everyone Listed In 1a, 1b, or 1c
In the narrative section, provide this information for everyone listed even if they are volunteers who receive no compensation (which is the norm for new organizations just getting started). If you are not sure of some of the information, give the most accurate information you can determine. If you have included a job description in your bylaws, you can simply state the page and paragraph where the job description exists for each position. If you have already listed the qualifications of the board members in the narrative, you can refer to that section instead of giving the same information again.

Line 3b: Common Control
This line is designed to disclose where control rests in an organization and if there are any other organizations exercising influence and control over your organization.

Here is an example: *Kid Care America of Rolla, Inc.* is a separate organization from *First Assembly of God-Rolla*, but the church pays part of the salary for the program director and provides facilities for the after-school program for at-risk kids. This information had to be disclosed in the Form 1023.

IRS instructions for Form 1023 define common control as:

"You and one or more other organizations have (1) a majority of your governing boards or officers appointed or elected by the same organization(s), or (2) a majority of your governing boards or officers consist of the same individuals. Common control also occurs when you and one or more commonly controlled organizations have a majority ownership interest (I am adding for clarity: more than 35%) *in a corporation, partnership, or trust."*

Line 4a, b, and c: Compensation-Setting Practices
"Yes" to all three of these questions means that you are using good judgment and practices in establishing compensation for your higher-level officers, and also means IRS is not concerned with these items. If you answer "No" to any of these, put an explanation in the narrative.

Lines 4d, e, f, g: How Do You Set Reasonable Compensation and How Do You Document It?
If you arrived at your compensation by making a comparison of other nonprofit and profit companies of similar size and function, and you documented how you arrived at the compensation in your board meeting minutes, then you can answer "Yes." If your board is not compensated, then you have no problems with this question. Just answer "Yes."

If you answer "No" to any of these questions, you must include an explanation in the narrative of how you arrived at reasonable compensation for your top officials. Excessive compensation can result in loss of tax-exempt status. What is excessive? Paying more than the

EXCESSIVE COMPENSATION CAN RESULT IN LOSS OF TAX-EXEMPT STATUS.

actual work accomplished for the amount paid when compared to similar positions in other nonprofits of similar size and budget. How do you know? This information is disclosed in tax returns, and tax returns for nonprofits are public records. You can also call similar nonprofits and ask.

Lines 5a, b, c: Conflict of Interest Policy
If you have adopted a conflict of interest policy similar to the example given in Chapter 12, check "Yes" and move on. If you answered "No," you must answer lines 5b and 5c.

Lines 6a and 6b: Non-Fixed Compensation for Top Officials
If you answer "Yes" to either of these items, you have waved a huge red flag, and your tax-exempt status is not likely to be approved. If you are basing compensation on performance, percentages, revenue or bonuses, you are using non-fixed payments, and IRS looks for corruption and sees this as a way to spread the profits around to insiders.

Lines 7a and 7b: Purchasing Goods, Services, and Assets From Top Officials, Employees, Or Contractors
Another big red flag here if you answer "Yes." If you do purchase any goods, services, or assets from insiders, make sure you explain it well in the narrative and give the IRS agent enough details to be comfortable with the business arrangement. If you have a contract, provide a copy to IRS with the application.

Lines 8a, 8b, 8c, 8d, 8e, 8f: Leases, Contracts, Loans, and Agreements With Insiders
Answering "Yes" to 8a does not necessarily throw up a red flag unless the compensation is more than is customary for the services or facilities in question. Remember to provide copies of all documents and include an in-depth explanation in the narrative section.

Lines 9a, 9b, 9c, 9d, 9e, 9f: Leases, Contracts, Loans, and Agreements With Other Organizations in Which Your Officers, Directors, or Trustees Are Also Officers, Directors, or Trustees
This question looks to uncover any undue influence, or conflicts of interest, of officials who might also have influence or ownership (35% or more) in another organization that your organization will do business with. A "Yes" answer to 9a requires thorough explanation in the narrative section and copies of any documents involved.

CHAPTER 20

PART VI

YOUR MEMBERS AND OTHERS THAT RECEIVE BENEFITS FROM YOU

"When you have confidence, you can have a lot of fun. And when you have fun, you can do amazing things."
—Joe Namath

WHO WILL BENEFIT?

This part of the application seeks to find out how you are selecting your target group to assist, and aims to ferret out any selection process that benefits members or private interests instead of public interest. A good test is whether you know ahead of time the names of the people or organizations you will help. If so, you may not be a 501(c)(3) public charity, but a private foundation instead.

Line 1a: Benefits to Individuals

If your nonprofit organization will be helping individuals directly, check "Yes" and describe your programs and how you will carry them out. Make sure to emphasize that your target individuals are from a class of people (such as poor, disabled, homeless, or senior citizens), not specific individuals you can name ahead of time. It is permissible to help specific individuals as long as you do not limit your services to specific people, and leave the opportunity to add others in the future whose name you do not even know yet. If you will be helping individuals only indirectly through other organizations, check "No" and move on.

Line 1b: Benefits to Organizations

If you provide goods and services to organizations, tell what programs will you offer and how you will carry them out. Make sure to emphasize that your target organizations are from a class of organizations (such as orphanages, hospitals, schools, senior citizen homes, etc.), not specific organizations that you can name ahead of time. It is fine to begin operations helping specific organizations, but make sure your narrative reflects the desire and opportunity to add other similar organizations at a later date. If not, IRS may declare you a private foundation instead of a public charity.

> MAKE SURE TO EMPHASIZE THAT YOUR TARGET ORGANIZATIONS ARE FROM A CLASS OF ORGANIZATIONS.

Line 2: Program Limits

Answering "Yes" to this item is another big red flag for IRS. If you limit your scope to specific individuals or specific organizations, you do not meet the requirement for 501(c) (3) status. You cannot select specific people or organizations ahead of time to the exclusion of all others who might be in that class or group. If you do, then you are not a true public charity. For example, if you plan to help one specific school, orphanage, or similar organization, make sure you include the possibility of working with other schools, orphanages, or organizations in the future, even if you only plan to work with one organization right now. Exception: IRS has been good about approving booster clubs, PTOs, and similar organizations for specific amateur sports teams and schools without including expansion in the long-term mission.

Line 3: Services to Relatives of Insiders
"Yes" to this question is another red flag to IRS. If the answer is yes, you must disclose it. Give a detailed explanation in the narrative.

CHAPTER 21

PART VII

YOUR HISTORY

"The person who says it cannot be done should not interrupt the person who is doing it."

—Chinese Proverb

This section tells whether your organization was formed from a previous organization and whether you have filed for 501(c)(3) status within 27 months of filing your state incorporation (Articles of Incorporation).

Line 1: Are You a "Successor" To Another Organization?
If you answer "Yes," it means that you have taken over all the assets or activities of another organization, been converted or merged from another organization, and/or have the same officials as another organization which doesn't exist anymore but previously served the same function. The previous organization could have been a tax-exempt organization but did not have to be.

An example from my town comes to mind. Twenty or so years ago, there was an organization called *LOVE* (Local Organization of Various Enterprises) that assisted people who had difficulty paying utility bills in winter, buying food, and paying rent. *LOVE* was closed, and the organization was converted to another organization called *GRACE* (Greater Rolla Area Charitable Enterprises). It became a one-stop facility for anyone who needed help with living expenses or food.

Local churches and helping organizations send everyone to *GRACE* first, and records are kept there of who received what help from where and when they received it. This has stopped abuse of people going to every helping organization in the area without disclosing that they already received similar help from a different local organization.

United Way lets residents contribute to *GRACE*, and local schools have canned food drives at holidays to assist *GRACE* in its mission. So, *GRACE* was the successor of *LOVE*, and in this case, both were nonprofit tax-exempt organizations.

If you answer "Yes," you must complete Schedule G of the application.

Line 2: 27 Month Time Limit to File for Tax-Exempt Status
IRS gives you up to 27 months to file Form 1023 after the state effective date for your Articles of Incorporation. If you file within that time, your tax-exempt status is made retroactive so that there is no gap in 501(c)(3) coverage. If you miss the 27-month deadline, your application can be approved, but will only be effective from the date of the postmark on the application. This could cause a problem for your donors because their donations would not be deductible before the postmarked date. You can request a waiver, but there is no guarantee you will get it.

If you did not file within 27 months, you need to fill out and attach Schedule E to the application. You might be eligible for 501(c)(4) status for the time that does not qualify for 501(c)(3) status, but that requires you include Form 1024, page 1 with your Form 1023. Best and easiest to file within the 27-month window.

CHAPTER 22

PART VIII

SPECIFIC ACTIVITIES

*"If you do what you've always done,
you'll get what you've always gotten."*

—Tony Robbins

Line 1: Do You Support or Oppose Candidates in Political Campaigns In Any Way?

If you answer this question "Yes," you just wasted a lot of time and effort because 501(c) (3) organizations CANNOT engage in political activities that endorse or oppose candidates. Period. End of Conversation. NO EXCEPTIONS.

Involving yourself in any political activity can be hazardous to your tax-exempt status. Because rightly dividing the regulations can be tricky, it is best to call IRS and discuss any proposed activities with them before you engage in them so as not to jeopardize 501(c) (3) status eligibility. The number is 877-829-5500. Call early in the day to avoid a recording that they are too busy to talk with you.

Line 2a: Do you attempt to influence legislation?

This is yet another fine line to navigate. If you answer "Yes," that means you are trying to persuade people to support or oppose legislation. You must give an explanation in the narrative that spells out how much time and money you are spending on influencing legislation. Tax exempt organizations are not allowed to engage in "substantial legislative activities." Although "substantial" is not well defined, case law has shown over time that 5% of time and money is NOT substantial, while 16% is considered substantial.

This is a tricky area. If you answer "Yes," you may want to contact a professional to assist you with meeting the requirements of the Internal Revenue Code and applicable Treasury regulations. Failure to abide within the parameters can result in loss of tax-exempt status, not getting tax-exempt status in the first place, and excise taxes being levied against the organization.

> FAILURE TO ABIDE WITHIN THE PARAMETERS CAN RESULT IN LOSS OF TAX-EXEMPT STATUS.

Line 2b: Form 5768, Election/Revocation of Election by an Eligible Section 501(c) (3) Organization To Make Expenditures To Influence Legislation

If you answered yes to line 2a, you may elect to have your activities to influence legislation calculated by how much you spend based on section 501(h). See Publication 557 for more details. Churches and private foundations are not allowed to complete Form 5768.

Lines 3a, 3b, 3c: Bingo

If you are going to conduct Bingo games or have them conducted on your behalf, answer these questions to fit your plans and circumstances. Provide details in the narrative. Remember that winners of high stakes Bingo games must be reported to IRS so the government can collect the taxes due on the winnings. If you are not going to engage in Bingo in any facet, mark "No," and move on.

Lines 4a, 4b, 4c, 4d, 4e: Fundraising
Whatever you put here must be explained and described, and it's a good idea to include copies of any paperwork you use with the application. If you are contemplating a certain type of fundraising but have not firmed up specifics or undertaken that mode of fundraising yet, you might want to leave it off the applicaiton. Put only what you are actually doing or will actually do in the near term.

The more you include, the more justification and paperwork you need, and the more chance that something will be questioned. I do not advocate leaving out any material information. Be honest and complete, but leave your future plans to the future, especially if you have not ironed out enough details to pass IRS scrutiny at the time of this application. Make sure this line agrees with Part IX, Financial Data.

You should be aware that IRS will look hard at any applicant who plans to use professional fundraisers. Due to frequent abuse of donor-advised accounts for personal gain, IRS also looks hard at organizations who plan to use them, and you may be subject to excise tax or not be granted 501(c)(3) status. Contact IRS to discuss your specific situation.

Here are some descriptions I have used, and IRS has accepted for this section:

> **Personal solicitation:** We intend to raise funds from individuals, groups, churches, and businesses by direct contact and through our website. We will invite individuals and groups with a commitment to our purposes and efforts to contribute to our organization. We do not have printed materials or brochures at this time. All donations will be solicited and recorded according to IRS codes.
> **Foundation grant solicitation:** We intend to raise funds by applying for foundation grants from organizations that support the type of services we are providing.
> **Governmental grant solicitation:** We intend to raise funds by applying for government grants that support our efforts.
> **Accept donations on your website:** We intend to raise funds on our own website once it is up and running.

Line 5: Government Unit Affiliation

Government units are not normally eligible for 501(c) (3) status because they have power to establish, control, manage, and/or supervise legal or government issues. However, some organizations, such as municipal hospitals, are affiliated with government units or Indian Tribal Governments and are eligible because they do not have those powers, or because they lessen the burden on the government. Google "Organizations Closely Affiliated with State or Indian Tribal Governments Reference Guide" for more information.

If you answer "Yes," include an explanation in the narrative. If not, check "No" and move on.

Lines 6a and 6b: Economic Development

Organizations created to counter deterioration of neighborhoods that have been recognized by a government agency as economically depressed, deteriorating, or blighted, qualify for 501(c) (3) status as economic development organizations. The services provided can be loans, grants, sharing knowledge, skill, business plans, or other business development tasks. Services can also include creation of industrial parks as well as to aid in eliminating prejudice and discrimination, or to decrease government burdens through business development.

IRS instructions for completing Line 6a include the following guidance:

> *"If your exempt purpose is to combat community deterioration, describe whether the area or areas in which you will operate have been declared blighted or economically depressed by a government finding. If the area has not been declared blighted or economically depressed, a more suitable exemption may be under sections 501(c) (4) or 501(c) (6). See Publication 557 for more information.*
>
> *If your exempt purpose is to eliminate prejudice and discrimination, describe how your activities further this purpose.*
>
> *If your exempt purpose is to lessen the burdens of government, describe whether the government has recognized your activities as those for which it would otherwise be responsible, and any involvement*

you have with governmental entities that demonstrates that you are actually lessening governmental burdens."

For Line 6b in the narrative, include a complete description of your target audience and how your services will fulfill exempt purposes.

Lines 7a, 7b, 7c: Development and Management Relationships
Once again IRS is looking for abuse or situations in which insiders and their families, friends, and business associates unfairly benefit or profit from affiliation with a tax-exempt organization. If any of these apply, full disclosure is required in terms of explanation, description of services, and copies of all agreements and contracts. You must explain how compensation was arrived at and how you ensured it was reasonable for services rendered or to be completed. Expect IRS scrutiny if you answer "Yes" to these.

Line 8: Joint Ventures
This item seeks to establish whether your tax-exempt organization plans to join forces for purposes of creating profit, with other individuals or organizations that are not 501(c)(3) approved. IRS instructions for this line define a joint venture as:

"a legal agreement in which the persons jointly undertake a transaction for mutual profit. Generally, each person contributes assets and shares risks. Like a partnership, a joint venture can involve any kind of business transaction and the persons involved can be individuals, companies, or corporations."

A nonprofit that I founded (*Pasture Valley Children Missions*, EIN 35-2468924) entered a joint venture with a local pharmacy to provide a market for jewelry made by women in Swaziland through the Bambanani Project. The agreement called for a 20% commission (the pharmacy's standard commission) on all items sold. This is the type of agreement that would need to be disclosed and explained if known or planned at the time of application. As it turned out, no commission was actually ever charged. The pharmacy donated the commission to the organization instead.

The same type of agreement was made with another organization to market the jewelry, but no disclosure was required because the second organization was also a tax-exempt organization.

This is a tricky area, and I highly recommend you talk with IRS about it if you have any joint ventures in force or planned with organizations that are not tax exempt.

Lines 9a, 9b, 9c, 9d. Childcare Organizations
Two choices exist for tax exemption here. You can be tax exempt as a childcare facility if you are classified as a school under Internal Revenue Code 170(b) (1) (A) (ii) which reads:

> *"an educational organization which normally maintains a regular faculty and curriculum and normally has a regularly enrolled body of pupils or students in attendance at the place where its educational activities are regularly carried on."*

If this applies to your organization, complete Schedule B of the application in addition to the Form 1023.

The second choice is a 501(k) childcare organization. You can qualify under Section 501(k) if the kids come to your location, you are allowing a parent to work or seek work, and you serve the general public. If you are only serving a specific employer or group, you are not eligible for 501(c) (3) status. At least 85% of those families you serve must meet these conditions, or you must describe how you are going to meet the requirement and increase the percentage to 85% to be eligible for tax-exempt status. Details are available at *https://www.irs.gov/pub/irs-tege/eotopich89.pdf*

Line 10: Intellectual Property
IRS instructions say that intellectual property includes patents for inventions; copyrights (for literary and artistic works such as novels, poems, plays, films, musical works, drawings, paintings, photographs,

sculptures, architectural designs, performances, recordings, film, and radio or television programs); trade names, trademarks, and service marks (for symbols, names, images, and designs); and formulas, know-how, and trade secrets.

Intellectual property also includes any written materials either published, printed, copied, or displayed on a website online. If you have a slogan or a logo, this is also intellectual property. If you are just starting out and have none of these yet, answer "No."

If you have developed any educational materials, brochures, or websites or any intellectual property from the ones listed above, you must answer "Yes," and give complete details on all items required for this line.

Here is my best guidance based on experience: If you personally have developed intellectual property, keep the rights to that property, but allow the nonprofit to use the materials you developed. Why? Because if you *give* it to the nonprofit and the nonprofit closes, you cannot have it back. You must give it to another nonprofit. If you *loan* it to the nonprofit, or *lease* it to the nonprofit, you still own it and if the nonprofit closes, you still own it and do not have to give it to another nonprofit. This can include books, domains, programs, trademarks, logos, and other items of intellectual property.

Line 11: Contributions of Real Property

Although cash is real, real property is anything but cash. IRS is concerned about scams and abuse in this area. The main areas of concern are how some are overvaluing the property for tax deduction purposes, and who has actual control of the contributed item. Answer "Yes" or "No" and explain what you will accept if the answer is "Yes."

I caution you not to put your land, buildings, or vehicles in the organization's name. Once the nonprofit owns them, you cannot have them back even if the nonprofit closes. All property must be given to another nonprofit. You can let the nonprofit use it or lease it and still maintain ownership, but if you give up your ownership claim (title, deed, etc.) to the nonprofit, it is gone forever, and you cannot get it back. In the case of vehicles, if you use your vehicle for organization business, the board can vote to reimburse your expenses using actual costs from receipts you provide, or on a mileage basis. For any mileage or driving expenses the organization does not reimburse, an individual can use the IRS mileage deduction rates:

Beginning on Jan. 1, 2017, the standard mileage rates for the use of a car (also vans, pickups or panel trucks) will be:

- *53.5 cents per mile for business miles driven, down from 54 cents for 2016*
- *17 cents per mile driven for medical or moving purposes, down from 19 cents for 2016*
- *14 cents per mile driven in service of charitable organizations*

Taxpayers always have the option of calculating the actual costs of using their vehicle rather than using the standard mileage rates.

Lines 12a, b, c: Operating in Foreign Countries
If you have operations in foreign countries, you need to explain the locations, operations, and how those operations promote or advance your tax-exempt purpose. You may want to read *https://www.irs.gov/pub/irs-tege/eotopic92.pdf* which summarizes previous revenue rulings about conducting foreign operation although you are a U. S. charity. It is allowed, and you can quote the revenue rulings in your narrative as support for your foreign operations.

Although tax deductions are not permitted for giving to foreign charities, people and businesses can donate to a U.S. 501(c)(3) approved organization that gives to foreign charities. Ever since the tragedy of 9/11, funneling money into terrorist activities has been a concern. You may want to explicitly state that your organization has no ties to terrorist activities, that you will abide by the Office of Foreign Assets Control (OFAC) guidelines and use the Blocked Persons list, and that all foreign operations are for tax-exempt purposes within the letter and the intent of Section 501(c)(3) of the Internal Revenue Code.

Line 13a, 13b, 13c, 13d, 13e, 13f, 13g:
Distributions to Organizations
If you make grants, loans, or distributions to organizations, you need to answer each part of this section and include copies of all forms you use in deciding who is eligible for a distribution, how much they get, and how you will monitor the funds to make sure they are being used for exempt purposes.

You also need to describe how you will keep records and what reports you will require. If there is a relationship between you and the grantee, you must disclose the details in your narrative.

Here is an acceptable way to answer Line 13e (you can borrow these words if they apply):

> *(Organization) will maintain its financial records on QuickBooks or similar software in accordance with general accounting principles for nonprofit organizations. Cash received is applied to Accounts Receivable Ledger and cash distributed is recorded in the Accounts Payable ledger. Likewise, organizations that receive distributions are required to maintain general accounting records and are required to report on a regular/monthly basis as to how, when, and where funds are applied.*

Lines 14a, 14b, 14c, 14d, 14e, 14f:
Distributions to Foreign Organizations
If you distribute funds to foreign organizations, you must explain to IRS how you make sure the money is going for tax-exempt purposes. As you answer the questions in this section, you may want to include a statement in the narrative that states if the organizations you are distributing to were located in the United States, they would qualify for 501(c) (3) status because their purposes are consistent with Section 501(c) (3). You might also want to state that you will follow guidelines established in *Voluntary Best Practices for U. S.-Based Charities.*

Line 15: Do You Have a Close Connection to Any Other Organization?

This is another item designed to detect undue influence or abuse. IRS instructions for this item specify that a close connection exists if:

> *You control the organization or it controls you through common officers, directors, or trustees, or through authority to approve budgets or expenditures. You and the organization were created at approximately the same time and by the same persons. For example, you were formed within months of the time that a social welfare organization and a political action committee were established by the same persons who were instrumental in your formation.*
>
> *You and the organization operate in a coordinated manner with respect to facilities, programs, employees, or other activities. For example, you share rental expenses for office space and employees with a for-profit corporation.*
>
> *Persons who exercise substantial influence over you also exercise substantial influence over the other organization and (1) you either conduct activities in common or (2) have a financial relationship. For example, a voting member of your governing body is also a voting member of the governing body of a business league with which you intend to cooperate in planning an advertising campaign that will inform the public about the benefits of a particular program. For example, a voting member of your governing body is also a voting member of the governing body of a business league that has made a loan to you.*

A tax-exempt organization can have a close connection to another tax-exempt organization, and it is not an issue. Both are 501(c) (3) approved, so it is fine for them to share facilities, have some of the same people involved in both organizations, and share some expenses of conducting tax-exempt activities.

Line 16: Cooperative Hospital Service Organizations
Section 501(e) lists operations that fall under the heading of cooperative hospital service organizations. They include data processing, purchasing, warehousing, billing and collection, food, clinical, industrial engineering, laboratory, printing, communications, record center, and personnel services. Only a narrow percentage of 501(e) organizations can make the cut to get 501(c) (3) status. If you answered "Yes" to this item, call IRS and discuss the specifics before submitting your application.

Line 17: Cooperative Service Organizations of Operating Educational Organizations
These organizations perform collective investment services for educational organizations. IRS Publication 557 advises that if answer "Yes" to this item, call IRS and discuss the specifics of your eligibility for 501(c) (3) status because this type of organization falls under Section 501(f) but the Form 1023 is still used to apply.

Line 18: Charitable Risk Pool
This type of organization provides insurance. If that describes you, contact IRS and discuss the details to determine if you are eligible for tax-exempt status. The IRS website lists the following criteria for exemption:

A charitable risk pool is treated as organized and operated exclusively for charitable purposes if it:

1. *Is organized and operated only to pool insurable risks of its members (not including risks related to medical malpractice) and to provide information to its members about loss control and risk management,*
2. *Consists only of members that are section 501(c) (3) organizations exempt from tax under section 501(a),*
3. *Is organized under state law authorizing this type of risk pooling,*
4. *Is exempt from state income tax (or will be after qualifying as a section 501(c) (3) organization),*
5. *Has obtained at least $1,000,000 in startup capital from nonmember charitable organizations,*

6. *Is controlled by a board of directors elected by its members, and*
7. *Is organized under documents requiring that:*

   a. *Each member be a section 501(c) (3) organization exempt from tax under section 501(a)*
   b. *Each member that receives a final determination that it no longer qualified under section 501(c) (3) notify the pool immediately, and*
   c. *Each insurance policy issued by the pool provide that it will not cover events occurring after a final determination described in (b).*

Line 19: Do You or Will You Operate a School?
You have extra paperwork to submit if you are applying for 501(c)(3) status as a school, as well as proving you have a well-publicized nondiscrimination policy. IRS defines a school as:

"an educational organization whose primary function is the presentation of formal instruction and which normally maintains a regular faculty and curriculum and normally has a regularly enrolled body of pupils or students in attendance at the place where its educational activities are regularly carried on."

This may include any level of compulsory education as well as higher education, trade and technical schools, and preschools or nurseries. In addition, schools that are part of museums, historical societies, or churches are also eligible. You must complete Schedule B and include it with your application. For specifics, read IRS Publication 557 beginning on page 24.

Line 20: Hospital or Medical Care
This type of organization treats medical conditions, including mental disability, either on an inpatient or outpatient basis. IRS recognizes rehab, mental health, and drug treatment centers; and medical education and research facilities as part of this category. You must complete Schedule C as part of your application. There are many rules for this category, and I suggest you call IRS and discuss the specifics before filing Form 1023.

Line 21: Elderly or Handicapped and Low-Income Housing
IRS instructions give the following definitions and guidance:

"Low-income housing" refers to rental or ownership housing provided to persons based on financial need.

"Elderly housing" refers to rental or ownership housing provided to persons based on age, including retirement, assisted-living, independent living, continuous care, and life care arrangements.

"Handicapped housing" refers to rental or ownership housing provided to persons based on physical or mental disabilities, including nursing homes. If you are a skilled nursing facility, you should also complete Schedule C.

This category has many rules to comply with, so I suggest you contact IRS and discuss your specifics before filing. You must also file Schedule F with your application. You may want to read the revenue ruling concerning elderly housing contained in this document: *http://www.irs.gov/pub/irs-tege/eotopicg04.pdf*

Line 22: Scholarships, Loans, and Grants
IRS instructions for this line include the following guidance:

- Answer "Yes" if you pay monies to an individual as a scholarship, fellowship, or educational loan, for travel, study, or other similar purposes. Also, answer "Yes" if you pay such amounts on behalf of an individual to a school or a tuition or educational savings program.
- Travel, study, or other similar purposes include payments made to enhance a literary, artistic, musical, scientific, teaching, or other similar capacity, skill, or talent of the individual recipient. For example, amounts paid to:

    a. Vocational high school students to be used to purchase basic tools.

b. Teachers to induce them to teach in an economically depressed, public school system.
c. A scientific researcher to underwrite that individual's research project.

Educational grants do not include amounts you pay to an individual as compensation, such as payments made to a consultant for personal services or to produce a report for you.

Educational grants do not include amounts paid to another organization that distributes your funds as a scholarship to an individual if you have no role in the selection process.

Additional IRS guidance for scholarships includes:

Scholarships. If the organization awards or plans to award scholarships, complete Schedule H of Form 1023. Also, submit the following:

1. *Criteria used for selecting recipients, including the rules of eligibility.*
2. *How and by whom the recipients are or will be selected.*
3. *If awards are or will be made directly to individuals, whether information is required assuring that the student remains in school.*
4. *If awards are or will be made to recipients of a particular class, for example, children of employees of a particular employer—*

   a. *Whether any preference is or will be accorded an applicant by reason of the parent's position, length of employment, or salary,*
   b. *Whether as a condition of the award the recipient must upon graduation accept employment with the company, and*
   c. *Whether the award will be continued even if the parent's employment ends.*

5. *A copy of the scholarship application form and any brochures or literature describing the scholarship program.*

CHAPTER 23

PART IX

FINANCIAL DATA

*"The question isn't who is going to let me;
It's who is going to stop me."*

—AYN RAND

THE MONEY

This section may seem difficult or tricky, but it does not have to be. IRS wants to know what has occurred financially to date with your organization, and/or what you expect to happen in the near future (the next few years). If you are a brand-new organization that has had nothing but minimal financial support or transactions, then this part is very easy to complete. Just remember that what you put in this section has to match the rest of the application including the narrative. IRS requires financial information for three years if you are less than a year old (this year, next year, and the year after), and four years if you are more than one year old (this year, and whatever combination of years past and future produces four years information).

The application filing fee is based on the actual (for organizations that have been around for a while) or projected (for new organizations just getting started) income of the organization.

If the average combined gross annual revenue is less than $10,000 per year, the filing fee is currently $400. If it is over $10,000 a year, the fee is $850. If you do not know what your revenues will be, give it your best educated guess. IRS will not penalize you for guessing too low (you don't have to go back and file again or pay more), and they will not give you a refund of filing fees if you guess too high. Do the best you can. A projection is a guess, a prediction, an estimate, and it is not binding on anything except the filing fee. Guess high, pay high. Guess low, pay low.

If you have been in operation more than a year and you are using a standard financial software program like QuickBooks, you can print the required reports and attach them instead of filling out the forms in Part IX. Simply write "See Attached" in any column for which you have a printed report, and place the reports behind the financial data page of the application so that the IRS agent won't have to look for them. The easier you make it for the agent, the less time and correspondence will be required to get your determination letter.

> A PROJECTION IS A GUESS, A PREDICTION, AN ESTIMATE, AND IT IS NOT BINDING ON ANYTHING EXCEPT THE FILING FEE.

You will need a statement of revenue and expenses (either actual, projected, or a combination of the two), and a balance sheet. That's it. If you choose to use the forms in the application, don't let the columns and categories overwhelm you. It's possible that much of it doesn't even apply to your organization. If a line doesn't apply to you, leave it blank or put zero and move on.

EXAMPLE OF PAGE 9 (Line-by-line coverage of this form appears next in this chapter, but if you just want to get done, here is a place to start):
If you are a brand-new organization, have no revenues yet, have no clue what your income or expenses will be, and think they will be under $10,000, here is an example of how you might fill in the financial form on page 9:

1. For dates:
    Current year: Your incorporation effective date to the end of the fiscal year (normally 12/31 and the current year).
    Column 2: 01/01/next year to 12/31/next year
    Column 3: 01/01/year after next to 12/31/year after next

2. Revenues: Lines 1 (or 9 if you have service revenue such as day care center payments from parents, or tuition fees from martial arts classes, etc.), 8, 10, and 13:
    Column 1 for all four lines: 5,000
    Column 2 for all four lines: 7,000
    Column 3 for all four lines: 9,000
    Total column for all four lines: 21,000

3. Expenses: Lines 23 and 24
    Column 1: 4,500
    Column 2: 6,500
    Column 3: 8,500

4. Narrative description of Line 23:
    For this year Column 1:
        $500 filing fees to establish nonprofit and file with IRS
        $4,000 program services
    For next year Column 2:
        $6,500 program services
    For two years from now Column 3:
        $8,500 program services

Yes, feel free to borrow these numbers (or adjust them to fit) if they make sense to your organization. You're welcome!

Page 9 Line-by-Line:

If you have been in existence less than one year, this is going to be so easy! You get to make the whole thing up for three years, giving it your best effort to determine the most likely income and expenses. So, what if you don't know for sure? Give it your best shot. Start somewhere, and think it through. Don't stress out over it. Just do it! No penalty for being wrong, but be as accurate as you can, knowing full well you won't know the real numbers until after the fact. IRS knows it is not accurate, you know it is not accurate, but they make you do it anyway. So just do it.

YOU CAN DO THIS!

The financial part of this application has caused more anxiety than probably any other section. RELAX! It's just paperwork, one line at a time, so let's get started:

Line 1: Gifts, Grants, and Contributions Received (do not include unusual gifts)
Unusual grants are unexpected large sums received from a disinterested party. Because the amount is large, it can affect your organization's classification as a public charity which must be supported primarily by the general public. For this reason, grants like this are reported further down on the form on Line 12.

On line 1, you report gifts, grants, and contributions from various sources that help you accomplish your tax-exempt purpose. You also report government units helping you that provide a service or facility to the general public (as opposed to a specific group). If you receive revenue to complete a program or function for the general public (for example, if your organization is hired by someone or an organization), report it on this line. If you sell tickets to the general public as opposed to being hired for a fee to perform, that income goes on Line 9, Gross Receipts. If you are not sure which line to put the income on, contact IRS and ask before filling out the form.

Line 2: Membership Fees
Most charitable nonprofits do not have membership fees because they do not have members. Having board members is not the same as having memberships; do not confuse the concepts. If you do have members and you charge a membership fee to support the organization, put the total of the fees on this line. Do not include fees charged to members for anything except membership. Any other fees paid (such as for admission, merchandise, services, or use of facilities) are gross receipts, not membership fees, and get reported on Line 9.

Line 3: Gross Investment Income
Any income received from any investment (loans, rents, royalties, dividends, interest, etc.) is entered here.

Line 4: Net Unrelated Business Income
Do you have any income from unrelated business activity? Any income of which less than 85% of the labor was not completed by volunteers? Any income that did not have anything to do with your exempt purpose? You report it on line 4. Contact IRS or see Publication 598 if you need more information on this line (specifically Chapter 4) to figure the unrelated business income. You can access it a *http://www.irs.gov/publcations/p598/*

Line 5: Taxes Levied for Your Benefit
If the public paid any taxes on your behalf, include the amount collected here.

Line 6: Value of Services or Facilities Furnished by a Government Unit Without Charge (not including the value of services generally furnished to the public without charge)
Use the fair market value that would be charged for an organization that is not tax exempt.

Line 7: Any Revenue Not Otherwise Listed Above or on Lines 9 - 12 below. (Attach an itemized list)
In my opinion, this line should have come AFTER line 12 because you have to complete lines 9 - 12 before you can answer this one. If you have other forms of income that do not fit into one of the other categories, put them here. Itemize them, and give a brief description (less brief if you think IRS needs more details to avoid sending you a letter asking for more information). If in doubt, contact IRS and ask before entering it here.

Line 8: Total lines 1 – 7
Use a calculator and do every column, as well as a total of all columns in the far-right column.

Line 9: Gross Receipts from Admissions, Merchandise Sold, or Services Performed, or Furnishing of Facilities in Any Activity that is Related to Your Exempt Purposes (Attach itemized list)
Do not include amounts you have already included on other lines of this form. You only want to count the amounts once. If you received funds for the use of facilities that were not for the direct benefit of the general public, list them here. You must itemize and include what government agency paid you, the purpose of the payment, and the amount. If in doubt, contact IRS and see Publication 598 before filling out this line. You can access this publication at *http://www.irs.gov/publications/p598/*

Line 10: Total of lines 8 and 9
Enter the total of both lines in each column and combine the totals in the far-right column.

Line 11: Net Gain or Loss on the Sale of Capital Assets (Attach schedule and see instructions)
This is the format for the schedule referred to in this question (from the IRS website):

Figure 2. Part IX-A. Statement of Revenues and Expenses
Line 11. Net Gain or (Loss)

		Categories		
		(A) Real Estate	(B) Securities	(C) Other
1.	Gross sales price of assets (other than inventory) by category.			
2.	Less: Cost or other basis and sales expenses.			
3.	Gain or (loss). Subtract line 2 from line 1.			
4.	Net gain or (loss) - Add line 3 of columns (A), (B), and (C). Enter here and on Form 1023, Part IX - A. Statement of Revenues and Expenses, line 11.			

If this line applies to your organization, put the total amounts for each category (not an itemized list). Create this format as best you can to include all required information. No actual form exists, I just created this one from examples so you would not have to create one.

Line 12: Unusual Grants
Did you unexpectedly receive a large grant from an uninterested party? This is where you record it. You must also completely describe your unusual grant in Part X, line 7. More information is available in Publication 557 which can be accessed at *https://www.irs.gov/pub/irs-pdf/p557.pdf*

Line 13: Total Revenue. (Add lines 10-12)
Add each column, put in the total, and also the cumulative total for each row in the far-right column.

Line 14: Fundraising Expenses
What are you spending (or plan to spend) on fundraising? If you hire a professional fundraiser, you must disclose the amount paid here as well. Attach a copy of the fundraising contract if you have one. Fundraising income should be included as part of the amount you listed on Line 1. This line is to show how much you spent to raise funds.

Line 15: Contributions, Gifts, Grants, And Similar Amounts Paid Out (Attach itemized list)

If you paid out or plan to pay out funds to people or organizations as part of your mission, then IRS needs the details. Who received the funds? How much? What for? If disclosing the name of the individual receiving the payout violates privacy provisions (such as names of those who receive scholarships), then lump the totals together and list them by program or category instead of by person. If you are not paying out directly to individuals or organizations, but instead providing goods or services to individuals or organizations, then don't include the amounts here; include them as program services on Line 23.

Line 16: Disbursements To Or For The Benefit Of Members (Attach an itemized list)

If you disbursed funds to members of your organization, a full disclosure of who, how much, and why is required. IRS instructions for this form say not to include any amount already included in Line 15. Make sure to explain this item completely. Exempt organizations under Section 501(c) (3) exist to benefit the public, not their members, so this area can be a little tricky. If in doubt, contact IRS and talk with them about your specifics before filling out this line.

Line 17: Compensation of Officers, Directors, and Trustees

In Part V of the application, you were asked to list the officers, directors, and trustees and their compensation. Make sure the information provided here matches the information given there. Enter the totals for all columns. You normally do not compensate board members. Reimbursing out-of-pocket expenses that board members incur while on organization business is not considered compensation.

Line 18: Other Salary and Wages

Do you have any employees who are not officers, directors, or trustees? Enter the totals paid to them (or planned in the future) in all columns. If you don't know, don't have funds to pay anyone, and have no idea how much you will be able to pay, just leave it blank. You can add employees when funds are available by voting on hiring at any board meeting, at any time in the future, when you are financially able to fund hiring an employee.

Line 19: Interest Expense
How much interest did you pay, if any? Do not include mortgage interest if it is being reported as part of occupancy expense on Line 20.

Line 20: Occupancy
Utilities, mortgage interest, real estate taxes, janitorial services, rent, electricity, heat, etc. This includes all facilities for which you pay these expenses to complete your exempt purpose.

Line 21: Depreciation and Depletion
These are calculated the same way they would be in a for-profit organization; the same rules apply. If in doubt, contact IRS and ask before filling in this line.

Line 22: Professional Fees
Accounting, consulting, legal counsel, contract management, and other fees paid to people or organizations who are not your employees. Do not include professional fundraising fees here that you have already reported on Line 14. Independent contractor fees would be reported on this line.

Line 23: Any Expense Not Otherwise Classified, Such As Program Services (Attach itemized list)
If you have expenses that were not included elsewhere on the form, combine the totals here, and make an itemized list. Examples of expenses that may not be included above could be the IRS filing fee for the Form 1023, the cost of this book, postage, telephone service (if not included in occupancy above), vehicle expenses, insurance payments, website fees, even bank charges can be included here. This is the catch-all line very much like the one at the end of Schedule C of Form 1040 for business owners. This is where you list the cost to run specific programs (program service fees). For example, suppose your tax-exempt purpose is to run an

afterschool program for at-risk kids. Your program services fees would include the cost of snacks, sports equipment, materials, and anything else you need to operate the program. You can lump them together as program service fees in the narrative, or you can break them down into snacks, sports equipment, etc. Your choice.

Line 24: Total Expenses (Add Lines 14 -23)
Total the expenses in all columns used. If you are a new nonprofit incorporating in the same year as you are filing the Form 1023, you will not use column 4. Also remember to total all rows.

BALANCE SHEET

A balance sheet is a financial statement that states the net worth of a business on a specific date. It includes the assets and the liabilities. If your financial software can create a balance sheet, you can print it and attach it behind this section. Just be sure to write "See Attached" on this section of the application. If not, use the form in the application.

IRS wants to know the net worth as of the last day of the most recently completed fiscal year. If your tax year ends in December, then the date IRS wants to know about is December 31 of last year. This is great news for a new nonprofit that did not exist on December 31 last year. Every line gets a zero, and you are ready to move on.

If your organization did exist as of the last day of your most recently completed fiscal year, then the information you provide should reflect the status as of that last day of the fiscal year.

ASSETS

Line 1: Cash
Combine all short-term assets (less than one year until maturity) and put in the total. This includes cash, petty cash, money in checking and savings accounts, money markets, certificates of deposit, treasury bills, etc.

Line 2: Accounts Receivable, Net
Unpaid accounts that you expect to collect from sales or services, minus any reserve for bad debts. Most nonprofits have no accounts receivable.

Line 3: Inventories
What do you have on hand that you bought, or made, and are either going to use or sell in the future? What is the inventory worth after you subtract the cost to produce or acquire it? Most nonprofits have no inventory.

Line 4. Bonds and Notes Receivable (Attach an itemized list)
This item is for bonds or notes your organization issued that you expect to be repaid. The itemized list needs to include the borrower's name, what the form of the obligation is and a description, the rate of return, when it is due, and how much is due. Most organizations do not have Bonds and Notes Receivable.

Line 5: Corporate Stocks (Attach an itemized list)
What is the fair market value of stocks your organization holds? The itemized list should include any stocks from closely-held corporations (those companies in which although the public owns some stock, most of it is held by a few people who have no plans to sell it). Include the name of the company, its capital structure, how many shares are held, and the fair market value. For stock listed on an exchange or sold in sufficient quantities over the counter to make it liquid, you must include the name of the company, the exchange, identify the stock and number of shares, and the fair market value. Most new nonprofits do not have any corporate stock, but sometimes someone donates stock to help the organization.

Line 6: Loans Receivable (Attach an itemized list)
If your organization made loans, either uncollateralized or mortgage loans, you must list each loan separately and who the loans were made to, the amounts, purpose, interest rates, and terms for how the loans

are being paid back. Total all the loans and put that amount on Line 6. Most new nonprofits do not have any loans receivable.

Line 7: Other Investments (Attach an itemized list)
This is where you list items such as government securities or properties held for investment. List them separately on an attached sheet and give the value of each. Most new nonprofits do not have investments.

Line 8: Depreciable and Depletable Assets (Attach an itemized list)
This is where you list items, equipment, or buildings not held for investment. Be sure to include the cost basis of the item in the itemized list. The cost basis is the original cost minus depreciation.

Line 9: Land
This is where you list land that the organization owns that is not for investment.

Line 10: Other Assets (Attach an itemized list)
Anything else the organization owns, including patents and intellectual property, gets a book value assigned and is listed here.

Line 11: Total Assets (Add lines 1 through 10)
Add them all up and put in the total.

LIABILITIES

Line 12: Accounts Payable
Include bills that need to be paid or are payable but not yet due. For example, suppliers, salaries, accumulated payroll taxes, and interest.

Line 13: Contributions, Gifts, Grants, Etc. Payable
What commitments have you made that you have not yet paid for? For example, are you obligated to a scholarship but have not written the check? This category includes commitments to individuals and organizations.

Line 14: Mortgages and Notes Payable (Attach an itemized list)
What are the balances due for notes and mortgages at the end of the current tax year/period? On the itemized list, show each note or mortgage, the lender, purpose, repayment terms, interest rate, and the original amount of the loan.

Line 15: Other Liabilities (Attach an itemized list)
If the organization owes anything else, put it here and list it on the attachment with sufficient detail to satisfy the IRS agent's curiosity.

Line 16: Total Liabilities (Add lines 12 through 15)
Put the total in on this line.

FUND BALANCES OR NET ASSETS

Line 17: Total Fund Balances or Net Assets
Assets - liabilities = fund balances, and may also be called net assets. For purposes here, if your software program uses fund accounting, report it. Otherwise, use only net assets which include capital stock, paid-in capital, retained earnings or accumulated income, and endowment funds. More details are available at *http://www.irs.gov/instructions/i990/ch02.html#d0e10850* by clicking on Part X.

**Line 18: Total Liabilities and Fund Balances
or Net Assets (Add lines 16 and 17)**
Put the total on this line.

**Line 19: Have There Been Any Substantial Changes in Assets
or Liabilities Since the End of the Period Shown Above?**
If "Yes," explain. Don't forget to explain why the change occurred.

Whew! Glad that is done!

Go have a cup of coffee or a latte or a sweet tea and relax. You earned it!

FINANCIAL REPORT

3.456
2.589
1.258
4.896

3.45   2.58   6.58   12.3

8.52   6.47
.58   6.02
56   7.43

CHAPTER 24

PART X

PUBLIC CHARITY STATUS

"Set your goals high, and don't stop till you get there."

—Bo Jackson

WHY YOU ARE A PUBLIC CHARITY

Part X is where you establish yourself as a public charity instead of a private foundation. For foundations, donations are only deductible up to 30% of adjusted gross income; public charity donations are deductible up to 50% of adjusted gross income. It is not the intent of this book to cover private foundations. If you are a private foundation, I suggest you consult IRS about your requirements.

At the beginning of this book, we looked at why you would be a public charity instead of a private foundation. In brief, your source of income in a private foundation does not come from the public, while a public charity's revenues do. To be a public charity, you must be a church, school, hospital, government unit, be testing for public safety, receive most of your support from the general public, or support other organizations that are public charities. Otherwise, you are a private foundation.

Line 1a: Are You a Private Foundation?
If you can answer "No" because you are a public charity, go to Line 5. A private foundation is one in which most of the support comes from predetermined sources such as a specific company or family. Private foundations pay some taxes on their investment income and cannot do as they want or invest where they want to. There are some restrictions that affect foundation operation, and with only a few exceptions, foundations must give away a percentage of their assets each year. Not so with public charities. Also, public charities are allowed to work directly with individuals; foundations must work through other 501(c) (3) organizations to accomplish their missions.

Line 1b: Mandatory Provisions
If you answer "Yes," to Line 1a, you are a foundation, and your organizing documents must contain the required language for tax-exempt eligibility, and you must include an explanation giving the location of these provisions in your documents.

Well over half the states require the mandatory provisions be included in the foundation's governing instruments. Details can be found in Revenue Ruling 75-038 located at *http://www.irs.gov/pub/irs-tege/rr75-038.pdf*

You can also see IRS *Publication 557, Chapter 3, Section 501(c) (3) Organizations, Private Foundations* for examples of required wording in organizing documents.

Line 2: Direct Involvement for the Active
Conduct of Tax-Exempt Purposes
If your foundation actually runs its own programs instead of contributes money to other organizations running tax-exempt programs, then you check "Yes," and continue the application. If "No," sign the application at the end of Part XI.

Line 3: Have You Existed for One Or More Years?
If "Yes," attach financial statements and sign Part XI. If no, continue.

Line 4: Attachments
If you have been around for less than a year, then you need proof or at least verification from an attorney of what your operations are and how you will fund them, and that they satisfy the requirements to be categorized as a private foundation. If you do not have an opinion of counsel, you can provide a statement giving the required information.

Line 5: Type of Public Charity.
Somewhere in the list for line 5, you will find the type that fits your charity. If unsure, contact IRS and ask them to help you decide.

- Many organizations select *5h* because they rely on the public for much of their support and they do not fall into some other category such as a church, school, hospital, or exist to support another tax-exempt organization. If you will depend on donations, grants, and contributions, select *5h*.
- Others select *5i* if most of the revenue for the nonprofit comes from program service fees charged or membership fees, etc. In other words, the organization is providing a service or membership of some kind, and that is where most of their revenues come from. If that is the case with your organization, select *5i*.

If you select 5a, 5b, 5c, or 5d, you have an additional schedule to complete. Instructions for these schedules are contained in the next section of this book.

If you select 5e, 5f, 5g, 5h, 5i, or 5j, you do not have any additional schedules to complete.

You can select 5j and let IRS decide what type of public charity you are. This will delay approval of tax-exempt status if they determine you are one of the categories that need to fill out an additional schedule.

For public charity status, there is a one-third public support test you must meet or a 10% facts and circumstance test. It's not that complicated:

- If at least one-third of your support comes from the public, you can have public charity status. Most organizations fall into this category.
- If between 10% and 33% comes from the public, but there are circumstances to be considered, then you may qualify under the facts and circumstances test. For more information, see IRS Basic Determination Rules at *http://www.irs.gov/pub/irs-tege/eotopicj93.pdf*

Lines 6a and 6b: Organizations Over 5 Years Old
Only complete these questions if you are more than five years old. If you are more than five years old, you have already completed the financial data and prior tax returns so that you can answer these questions.

Line 7: Unusual grants
If you are a brand new organization, you only need to mark No.

According to IRS,

"Unusual grants" generally are substantial contributions and bequests from disinterested persons that by reason of their size adversely affect classification as a public charity. They are unusual, unexpected, and received from an unrelated party. If you answer "Yes" to line 7, submit a statement for each grant. The statement should include the name of the contributor, the date and amount of the grant, a brief description of the grant, and an explanation of why it is unusual. You should include details of any additional funds you expect to receive from the contributors listed. If they qualify for unusual grant treatment, these amounts should be reported on Part IX-A. Statement of Revenues and Expenses, line 12."

CHAPTER 25

PART XI

USER FEE INFORMATION

"Money is only a tool. It will take you wherever you wish, but it will not replace you as the driver."

— AYN RAND

> **NOTE:** Most applicants do not need to complete any of the schedules after this part of the application. If you do, remember to continue to the next section. In either case, you have to pay the IRS filing fee for the application.

Your IRS filing fee is $600 payable to U. S. Treasury. In the box on page 11 that asks for user fee, type in $600.

An officer must sign the application. Print the officer's name and title, and date the application.

Put a check payable to *U. S. Treasury* in the IRS package (put your FEIN number in the memo) and place the check on top of the other documents. Do NOT staple the check to the application. The IRS agent scans the documents into their system, and it is irritating and time-consuming to remove paper clips, staples, and binder clips, so don't use any.

When you (meaning an officer, director, or trustee) sign the application, you are certifying that everything you are sending is true, correct, and complete to the best of your knowledge.

Mail your Form 1023 and all required attachments to:

Internal Revenue Service
Attention: EO Determination Letters
Stop 31
P.O. Box 12192
Covington, KY 41012-0192

PART III
IRS SCHEDULES FOR TAX-EXEMPT STATUS

CHAPTER 26

SCHEDULE A
CHURCHES

"You must be the change you want to see in the world."
—Mahatma Gandhi

If it looks like a church, acts like a church, and functions like a church, it is probably a church. This classification includes mosques, temples, synagogues, etc. There must be a congregation or other membership. The church must have a denomination. Nondenominational churches may be granted religious organization 501(c)(3) status, but not church status.

IRS has some specific attributes it looks for to determine if you are a church according to their definition. You do not need to have all these attributes, but if some are missing that are typical for a church, or if the congregation is very small, it may create some thought of fraud or misrepresentation in the IRS agent's mind. Below is the list of attributes according to IRS. You do not have to have all fourteen to qualify for church status. However, some are more important than others. The items with asterisks are normally expected for approval as a church. If you do not have these yet (such as a large enough membership), just wait until you can meet the requirements to file. Churches are automatically tax-exempt under Section 501(c) (3) of the Internal Revenue Code, so you never have to file. Many churches choose to file to assure their tithing members that their contributions are tax deductible. If you choose to file, wait until you are big enough to cover the necessary items below:

- *A distinct legal existence* (Are you incorporated with the state as a church?)
- *A recognized creed and form of worship* (Do you have a denomination? A statement of faith? A written creed? What does a worship service look like in terms of how you conduct it? Do you sing hymns? Give testimonies? Present sermons? Have altar calls? Exactly what is your form of worship?)
- *A definite and distinct ecclesiastical government* (Do you have a pastor or equivalent? Do you have a system of who is in charge, a board, trustees, etc.?)
- *A formal code of doctrine and discipline* (What is your doctrine and what do you do when someone violates tenets of that doctrine?)
- *A distinct religious history* (History of your church and your denomination)
- *A membership not associated with any other church or denomination* (With few exceptions, IRS expects that members {not just attendees} of your church belong only to your church or denomination)
- *Ordained ministers ministering to the congregation* (qualified religious leaders with qualifications depending on the norms of the denomination)
- *Ordained ministers selected after completing prescribed courses of study* (What training does your religious leader have? How did he or she become ordained, licensed, or otherwise qualified to be a church leader, pastor, bishop, etc.?)
- *A literature of its own* (The Bible or other religious literature qualifies)

- *Established place of worship* (Do you have a stable location to meet? It can be rented, leased, owned, or borrowed).
- *Regular congregations* (IRS looks for a minimum of 20-25 congregation members who have met membership requirements and have formally been accepted as members of the congregation. Not everyone who attends is a member. IRS wants a stable membership large enough to maintain a church. The congregation cannot be mostly one or two families; it must be from a number of families).
- *Regular religious services* (Do you have a schedule of service days and times that you follow?)
- *Sunday schools for the religious instruction of the young* (Do you provide religious training for children and youth?)
- *Schools for the preparation of ministers* (Do you have some type of discipleship program to grow new church leaders?)

Line 1a: Written Statement of Faith
Your denomination, written creed, statement of faith, or summary of beliefs must be attached.

Line 1b: Form of Worship
What are the practices of your church that show your dedication to your beliefs?

Line 2a: Code of Doctrine and Discipline
What laws or rules do you function under?

Line 2b: Religious History
Give an overview of how you came into being; tell your history and milestones. Also, include the history of your denomination.

Line 2c: Literature
Any writings containing practices, rules, laws, doctrines, history, as well as your religious book you teach from such as the Bible.

Line 3: Religious Hierarchy or Ecclesiastical Government
What is the chain of command?

Line 4a: Regularly Scheduled Religious Services
Give days of the week and times, the order of events, and an explanation of how these activities further your religious purpose. Include copies of church bulletins, pamphlets, or other printed material handed out to members or the public if you have any. If not, state that you have no printed materials.

Line 4b: Average Attendance
Very small numbers in attendance are suspect to IRS, especially if most of the members are from one or two families.

Line 5a and 5b: Established Place of Worship and Ownership
You do not need to own the location used to conduct services. You can rent it, or it can be provided to you at no charge. If you do not have a location, where are you meeting? Not having a location can cause IRS to downgrade you to a religious organization instead of giving you church status.

Line 6: Established Congregation
This means an established membership that includes people from more than one or two families. If you do not have an established membership yet, wait to file the application until you do or choose another public charity type on Part X, Line 5 of Form 1023. If in doubt, contact IRS and discuss your circumstances. Very small congregations are suspect to IRS.

Line 7: Number of Members
Enter the number of members. IRS is looking for a minimum of 20-25 members. Members are not the same as attendees. You can attend a church and not be a member. How many actual members do you have who have met your requirements for membership and have been accepted as members of your congregation?

Line 8a, 8b, 8c, and 8d: Process to Become a Member
Answer "Yes" if you keep records of who is currently a member. If all your members are from the same family, you are not classified as a church. Give IRS the details requested to determine how a person would become a member of your church and what the benefits of that membership would be. Attach a copy of an application if one exists. Don't create a membership application if you don't have one, IRS will approve you without one.

Line 9: Church Rites and Rituals Performed
These include weddings, baptisms, funerals, communion, and other rites. It is normal for churches to have these rights and rituals. You do not have to do all of these in every denomination. Explain in the narrative which ones you perform in your denomination. If you have not done them previously (such as weddings) but plan to, say so.

Line 10: Religious Instruction
Do you have regularly scheduled youth or children's educational activities such as Sunday school? Describe them the narrative.

Line 11a and 11b: Prescribed Course of Study
What training has your minister or religious leader completed? Self-ordination, self-study, or methods that did not include a formal course of instruction and learning do not qualify as a prescribed course of study. Some denominations have ordination boards. If yours is one, explain the process for your denomination.

Line 12: Is Your Religious Leader an Official in Your Church?
If the minister or other religious leader is listed in Part V, Line 1a, check "Yes."

Line 13: Do You Ordain, Commission, Or License Ministers?
If so, include an explanation of the requirements to be ordained, commissioned, or licensed. This is not common to all denominations.

Answering "No" does not decrease your chances of being approved as a church.

Line 14: Are You Part of a Group of Churches with Similar Beliefs and Structures?
Are you part of a convention, association, or union of churches? Include the name of the group you are part of. Most churches applying for 501(c) (3) status will answer "No." This question is not asking you if you are a Southern Baptist, or part of the Catholic church. It is asking if you fall under a parent organization's 501(c) (3) umbrella. If you are applying for your own 501(c) (3), then you will not be part of group exemption, you will have your own exemption.

If you are leaving a group exemption, then explain why you are leaving. I had one client who was a pastor of a Holiness church. The parent organization's doctrine stated that men could not wear neckties. Several members of this church's congregation were bankers, attorneys, and other professionals who had to wear a tie to work. The church filed for their own 501(c) (3) tax-exempt status and removed the restriction on neckties in their church constitution. That was their explanation for leaving the group exemption and getting their own exemption outside the umbrella of the parent organization.

Line 15: Do You Issue Church Charters?
If so, what are the requirements for issuing a charter? Most churches answer "No."

Line 16: Fee for Charter
If you paid a fee for a church charter, include a copy of the charter. Be sure to tell which organization provided the charter and their requirements. Do not include organizational charters from the Secretary of State, Franchise Tax Board, or other governmental administrative function. Most churches answer "No."

Line 17: Additional Information
Is there anything else you want IRS to know to decide if you qualify for tax exemption as a church? Attach it to the package or include it in the narrative. I suggest you answer this question like this (feel free to copy!):

> *We do not attempt to influence legislation or intervene in any way in political campaigns other than to vote our conscience on election days.*
>
> *We are not already exempt under a group-ruling letter of a parent organization, and are not part of a conference, convention, or association of churches.*
>
> *Under IRC § 508(c), churches are not required to apply for recognition of exemption with IRS to be treated as an organization described in IRC § 501(c) (3). We already meet the requirements without applying, but choose to seek formal recognition of exemption.*

IS THERE ANYTHING ELSE WE CAN DO TO HELP WITH CHURCH STATUS?

Glad you asked! In the narrative attachment to the application, sprinkle pictures throughout the package and the Schedule A narrative. Show the sanctuary (even if it is a store front leased unit), the outside of the building, the church sign, and a street view of the church showing a little of the neighborhood. If you have any pictures of worship services, the choir, Sunday school classes, or similar photos, include them in the narrative. A picture really is worth a thousand words to the IRS agent who is trying to envision your church and decide if it is a real church or a religious organization.

CHAPTER 27

SCHEDULE B

SCHOOLS, COLLEGES, AND UNIVERSITIES

"He who opens a school door closes a prison."
—Victor Hugo

Not all schools are created equal, and not all schools qualify for tax-exempt status. Your organization is only qualified if your main activity is conducting formal instruction, if you have scheduled habitual customary curriculum, qualified teachers, an identifiable student body taking classes on a regular basis, and there is an identifiable location for these classes and students to meet to conduct this formal, habitual, scheduled curricular instruction. Sounds like a mouthful, but it is IRS making sure you actually are conducting instruction, not running a diploma mill.

IRS definition of *school* includes "primary, secondary, preparatory, high schools, colleges, and universities." Homeschools do not qualify for tax-exempt status.

SECTION I:
OPERATIONAL INFORMATION

Lines 1a and 1b: Do You Qualify as a School?
If you can answer "Yes" to both questions, provide requested descriptions in the narrative and move on to the next question. If not, you are a school for tax-exempt purposes.

Lines 2a and 2b: Are You a Public School? If you can answer "Yes" to both questions, provide requested descriptions in the narrative and move on to Line 3. If not, do not fill out the rest of Schedule B.

Line 3: Your Location
What is the name of the public school district and county where you conduct instruction?

Lines 4, 5, and 6: Discriminatory Practices.
These questions seek to determine if you discriminate based on race, color, and national or ethnic origin. If you do, you do not qualify for tax-exempt status. Include a copy of your bylaws containing your nondiscrimination policy. If it is not included in your formal organizing or operating documents, include a copy of your signed resolution approving a nondiscrimination policy.

Line 7: Fair Market Value of Services
It is possible that if this applies to your school, you have already answered this question back in Part VIII, question 7. If so, you can reference that answer, but be sure to include any additional information requested that is not included in Part VIII.

Line 8: Who will manage your activities?
If you select "No," be sure to include all required documentation. You can reference Part VIII if you have already provided this information.

SECTION II:
ESTABLISHMENT OF RACIALLY NONDISCRIMINATORY POLICY

Revenue Procedure 75-50 located at *http://www.irs.gov/pub/irs-tege/rp1975-50.pdf* requires that you not only have a racially nondiscrimination policy but that you also publicize it. The statement that must be used is included in quotes in the next paragraph.

Revenue Ruling 71-447 located at *http://www.irs.gov/pub/irs-tege/rr71-447.pdf* clarifies what nondiscrimination means in terms of tax-exempt status,

> *"The _____ School admits the students of any race to all the rights, privileges, programs, and activities generally accorded or made available to students at that school and the school does not discriminate on the basis of race in administration of its educational policies, admissions policies, scholarship and loan programs, and athletic and other school-administered programs."*

In addition, nondiscrimination statements must be included in all brochures, advertisements, catalogs, and other printed materials given to the public and the student body. Don't forget to include it on internet pages. The exact wording IRS likes to see is:

> *"The _____ School admits students of any race, color, and national or ethnic origin."*

Line 1: Do You Have a Nondiscriminatory Policy in Effect?
If you do not, you must approve a resolution implementing one and attach evidence to this application that you have one in place. If not, you will be denied tax-exempt status.

Line 2: Is the Nondiscriminatory Policy Publicized in Your Documents?

If "Yes," attach a copy of one of your documents such as brochures or catalogs that show how you are marking your documents. If "No," that means you agree to put the policy in all future documents for the public or student body.

Line 3: Publication in a General Circulation Newspaper

You have to prove to IRS that the public knows you do not discriminate. The easiest way to meet this requirement is to publish the following statement in the newspaper annually. If you have done so, send the entire newspaper page with the application. No partial pages or copies from a copying machine are acceptable. The newspaper disclosure should read:

> "The _____ School admits the students of any race to all the rights, privileges, programs, and activities generally accorded or made available to students at that school and the school does not discriminate on the basis of race in administration of its educational policies, admissions policies, scholarship and loan programs, and athletic and other school-administered programs."

Specific guidance is available in Revenue Ruling 75-50, located at *http://www.irs.gov/pub/irs-tege/rp1975-50.pdf*

Line 5: Racial Composition

IRS wants numbers of students, not percentages. Do not include names of staff, faculty, or students, just the actual number (or projected number if you are just starting out) in each category. If you are estimating, you have to submit information explaining to IRS how you came up with the estimates. You can use census data for your area and estimate based on percentages from the census. If your numbers differ significantly from the census data submitted, you must explain why.

Line 6: Racial Composition for Loans and Scholarships
Use current year actual numbers and projected numbers for next academic year.

Line 7a and 7b: List of Those Who Were Instrumental in Starting The School And Whether They Want To Segregate
For 7a, provide a list of all incorporators, founders, board members, donors of land, and donors of buildings. Then in 7b, explain any circumstance in which any of those listed in 7a want to keep public or private education segregated by race. Schools that promote segregation are not eligible for tax-exempt status.

Line 8: Records for Three Years
Revenue Ruling 75-50 requires you to keep specific records if you want to get and keep tax-exempt status. You need to maintain records for a minimum of three years showing your school's racial composition, evidence that your scholarships and loans are awarded without discrimination, copies of solicitation materials for contributions, and copies of brochures, advertisements, application forms, catalogs, etc. If you plan to do that or are already doing it, answer "Yes." If "No" you must explain how you plan to meet these requirements.

CHAPTER 28

SCHEDULE C

HOSPITALS AND MEDICAL RESEARCH ORGANIZATIONS

*"Healing is a matter of time,
but it is sometimes also a matter of opportunity."*
—Hippocrates

If you are a cooperative hospital service organization, you do not need to fill out Schedule C. It is only used if you are a hospital or medical research organization operated in combination with a hospital. If the main function of an organization is medical treatment services, it qualifies as a medical care facility even though it may be operating on an outpatient basis. Treatment can be for physical or mental conditions and includes drug treatment centers.

The definition of *hospital* does not include convalescent homes, children's or elderly homes, or institutions providing job training for the handicapped.

According to IRS guidelines, a medical research organization is one whose *"principal purpose or function is the direct, continuous, and active conduct of medical research in conjunction with a hospital."* In addition, IRS requires that *"the research must be to discover, develop, or verify knowledge relating to the causes, diagnosis, treatment, prevention, or control of human physical or mental diseases and impairments."*

Hospitals must complete Section 1 of Schedule C. Medical Research Organizations must complete Section II.

SECTION I:
HOSPITALS

Line 1: Who Has Staff Privileges?
If all doctors in your area have staff privileges or are only restricted due to capacity, then mark "Yes." If "No," describe how you determine which courtesy staff have privileges at your facility and the exact criteria and selection procedures used.

Lines 2a, b, c: Insurance, Self-Pay, Medicare, and Medicaid
If you restrict admission in any of these categories, you must provide an explanation of how and why you restrict patient admittance to exclude any of these categories.

Line 3a and 3b: Medicare/Medicaid Deposits
If you require a deposit, how do you determine the amount, and why do you require it? Is a similar deposit required of patients who do not have Medicare or Medicaid? If not, why not? Describe in detail.

Lines 4a, 4b, and 4c: Emergency Services
What provisions do you have to treat emergencies when someone cannot pay? Do you have a written policy? Do you have written or verbal agreements with first responders concerning emergency services? Describe them and include copies of written policies and agreements. If

you have verbal agreements, explain them in detail to include how and when the agreements were made.

Lines 5a, 5b, 5c, 5d, 5e: Provisions for Charity Patients
Describe in detail how you handle charity patients.

Lines 6a and 6b: Medical Training and Community Education
Include details of how your program works and any organizational affiliations.

Line 7: Office Space to Physicians
If you lease to physicians, you must show IRS that you are getting fair market value for the space and provide representative copies of leases.

Line 8: Governing Boards
This question seeks to ascertain whether your board of directors is representative of the community where you are located. IRS instructions for this item give this exact guidance:

- Answer "Yes" if you have a board of directors that is representative of the community you serve. Include a list of each board member with the individual's name and employment affiliation. Also, for each board member, describe how that individual represents the community. Generally, hospital employees and staff physicians are not individuals considered to be community representatives.
- Answer "Yes" if an organization described in section 501(c) (3) with a community board exercises rights or powers over you, such as the right to appoint members to your governing board of directors and the power to approve certain transactions. Describe these rights and powers. In addition, describe how each of that organization's board of directors represents the community.
- Answer "Yes" if you are subject to a state corporate practice of medicine law that requires your governing board to be

composed solely of physicians licensed to practice medicine in the state. If you answer "Yes" on this basis, also provide the following information.

- Describe whether a hospital described in section 501(c)(3) exercises any rights or powers over you.
- Identify the corporate practice of medicine law under which you operate.
- Explain how the section 501(c)(3) hospital exercises any rights or powers over you, such as the right to appoint members to your governing board of directors and the right to approve certain transactions.
- Explain what services you provide to the section 501(c)(3) hospital.

Line 9: Joint Ventures
Make sure that if you participate in joint ventures, you answer each part of this question and your answers match Part VIII, Line 8.

Line 10: Managing Your Programs
If you contract the management of your programs, provide all requested information and make sure your answers match Part VIII, Line 7b.

Line 11: Physician Recruitment Incentives
It is okay to offer incentives to recruit physicians, especially in shortage areas. Disclose all incentives in detail.

Line 12: Do You Lease from Physicians Who Have a Financial or Professional Relationship with Your Hospital?
This question includes any physician you have a business relationship with: employees, staff physicians, those who are in a joint venture with you, or those you have service contracts with. How did you establish fair market value?

Line 13: Purchase from Business Colleagues
If you purchased an existing medical practice, supplies, equipment, or any other business asset from anyone you had a business relationship with, you must disclose it and how you established fair market value. Include copies of sales contracts and appraisals.

Line 14: Conflict of Interest Policy
If you do not have a conflict of interest policy in place, how do you avoid conflicts in business dealings? If you do have one, does it meet or exceed the IRS example? How did you adopt it: bylaws, resolution, etc.?

Having a conflict of interest policy is not required by tax law, but IRS looks at it as one more step to ensure that you are operating to benefit the community and not for private advantage or gain.

SECTION II:
MEDICAL RESEARCH ORGANIZATIONS

Line 1: Relationships with Hospitals
Provide a list of all hospitals you work with, describe the nature of the interaction and relationships, and attach copies of all agreements.

Line 2: Schedule of Activities
Whether actual or proposed, provide a schedule of your activities that directly support your medical research. Include the characteristics and features of the activities and how much money you are spending or will spend on each activity. According to IRS, making grants to other organizations is not an activity of your research.

Line 3: Assets
List your assets, their fair market value, and what percentage of each asset is being used for research.

CHAPTER 29

SCHEDULE D

SECTION 509(A) (3) SUPPORTING ORGANIZATIONS

LUCK: Laboring Under Correct Knowledge.

—Paul Crump

If you chose Part IX, line 5d, you have to complete Schedule D because you said you are an organization that only gives money to other nonprofit organizations. This is common when you are a supporting arm of an established tax-exempt organization that doesn't want to detract from its nonprofit mission to raise funds. So, you are the fundraising body that supports the other organization. This is permissible as long as you maintain control, but several possibilities exist that you may be controlled (in the eyes of IRS) by "disqualified persons."

Electing this schedule has many technical applications, and I strongly suggest you seek the help of a tax professional before filing to eliminate months of follow-up paperwork to meet the intent and the letter of the law for IRS. The technicalities are beyond the scope of this book. It is a book in itself and is worth every cent you spend to get a professional to complete this schedule. You may want to go back and see if this is the best selection under Part IX. If another less complicated selection is possible, you may want to choose it. However, if you are still sure you want to file Schedule D, here is some basic guidance and resources to figure out the technicalities. If in doubt, contact IRS and talk to them about your specific circumstances before filing.

First of all, you can qualify as a public charity under Section 509(a)(3) if you operate entirely to benefit, perform the functions of, or carry out the purposes of one or more public charities listed in Section 509(a)(1). This will include organizations that get their funding from a wide range of sources such as churches, schools, hospitals, etc. You can also qualify as a public charity if you exclusively benefit Section 509(a)(2) organizations, which include organizations that get their funds from grants, donations, or fees for their nonprofit purpose.

You can also qualify as a supporting organization if you are supporting the charitable purposes of 501(c)(4) organizations (civic leagues, social welfare organizations, local associations of employees), 501(c)(5) organizations (labor, agriculture, and horticultural organizations), or 501(c)(6) organizations (business leagues, chambers of commerce, and real estate boards).

You also must meet a relationship test, and not be controlled directly or indirectly by "disqualified persons" which are defined at *http://www.irs.gov/irm/part7/irm_07-027-020.html*

SECTION 1:
IDENTIFYING INFORMATION ABOUT SUPPORTING ORGANIZATIONS

Line 1: Organizations You Support
Write the name, address, and employer identification number (FEIN) of every organization you support. Attach another sheet of paper if you have more than will fit in the blanks.

Line 2: Are you supporting organizations under Section 509(a) (1) or 509(a) (2)?
If "Yes" go to Section II, Line 1. If "No," continue this section.

Line 3: Are Supporting Organizations Under Section 501(c) (4), 501(c) (5), or 501(c) (6)?
These organizations include 501(c) (4) organizations such as civic leagues, social welfare organizations, local associations of employees; 501(c) (5) organizations such as labor, agriculture, and horticultural organizations; and 501(c) (6) organizations such as business leagues, chambers of commerce, and real estate boards. If so, you need to provide the financial data requested or otherwise explain how they are a public charity under Section 509(a) (1) or 509(a) (2).

SECTION II:
RELATIONSHIP WITH SUPPORTED ORGANIZATION(S)—THREE TESTS

According to IRS, a supporting organization must meet at least one of these three tests:

Test 1: "Operated, supervised, or controlled by" one or more publicly supported organizations, or

Test 2: "Supervised or controlled in connection with" one or more publicly supported organizations, or

Test 3: "Operated in connection with" one or more publicly supported organizations.

Line 1: Governing Board or Officers
Test 1 ascertains whether most of the governing board or officers are elected or appointed by the supported organization(s). If "Yes," you must give an explanation of how they are appointed or elected. If "No," go on to the next question.

Line 2: Serving on More Than One Governing Board
Test 2 ascertains whether most of the governing board members also serve on the governing board(s) of the supported organization(s). If "Yes," you must give an explanation of how they are appointed or elected. If "No," go to the next question.

Line 3: Responsiveness Test. Test 3 ascertains whether you are a trust in which the supported organization(s) can force you to give an accounting under state law. If "Yes," explain and provide written proof that the supported organization(s) know they can make you give them an accounting. Then go to line 5. If "No," go on to the next question.

Lines 4a, 4b, 4c, 4d, 4e: Alternate Ways to Meet Test 3
These five items are designed to provide an alternate method of qualifying under test 3. Basically, IRS wants to know the nature and extent of working relationships you maintain with supported organization(s), and how much input they have into your procedures, investment decisions, and use of funds. All questions you answer "Yes" require documentation to substantiate.

Line 5: Activities
This line ascertains whether you are operated in connection with supported organization(s). If you conduct activities that would otherwise be carried out by the supported organizations if you did not do them, answer "Yes" and give an explanation and skip the rest of Section II. If "No," continue with Section II.

Lines 6a, 6b, 6c, 6d: Net Income Distribution
This item provides an alternate way to meet the integral part criteria of test 3. If you distribute at least 85% of your annual net income to supported organization(s), you may qualify for public charity status. Provide requested explanations and lists. If you answer "No" to 6a, and to line 5, you do not qualify for public charity status. Go back and rethink the status you selected in Part X of Form 1023 to see if another selection is more appropriate.

Lines 7a and 7b: Specifying Supported Organization(s)
Look at your organizational document (Articles of Incorporation for example). Did you name the supported organization(s) in it? If "Yes," give the article and paragraph number and go to Section III. Include requested explanation of relationship(s).

If you cannot answer "Yes," you may want to amend your organizing document unless you can provide evidence of historical or continuing relationship between your organization and the supported organization(s). If you cannot do either, you do not qualify as a public charity. Go back to Part X of Form 1023 and rethink your selection to see if another selection is more appropriate.

SECTION III:
ORGANIZATIONAL TEST

Lines 1a and 1b: Supported Organization(s) by Name
If you cannot answer "Yes," you do not qualify for public charity status. If you answered "No," you can go back and change your organizing documents. Otherwise, you do not meet the organizational test. You can still go back and change Part X of Form 1023 and select a different choice for public charity status eliminating the need to do Schedule D.

SECTION IV:
DISQUALIFIED PERSON TEST

Lines 1a, 1b, and 1c: Disqualified Persons
Organizations controlled directly or indirectly by disqualified people make the organization ineligible for public charity status. Section 4946 of the IRS code gives the following guidelines on who is a disqualified person:

- Substantial Contributor (normally more than $5,000 a year if that is more than 2% of the total contributions of the previous year)
- Foundation manager (includes officers, directors, and trustees)

- Owner of more than 20% interest in an organization that is a substantial contributor
- Family members. IRS defines family members to include an individual's spouse, ancestors, lineal descendants, and the spouses of his or her lineal descendants. Also, the legally adopted child of an individual is his or her child within the meaning of this regulation. Internal Revenue Code (IRC) 4946(d) provides that the family of any individual shall include only his spouse, ancestors, children, grandchildren, great grandchildren, and the spouses of children, grandchildren, and great grandchildren. Also includes the surviving spouse of a child, grandchild, or great grandchild of a substantial contributor (until remarriage).
- Persons who hold more than a 35% interest
- Government official

CHAPTER 30

SCHEDULE E

ORGANIZATIONS NOT FILING FORM 1023 WITHIN 27 MONTHS OF FORMATION

"One of the strongest characteristics of genius is the power of lighting its own fire."
—JOHN W. FOSTER

If you have been in existence for more than 27 months, you have some special filing rules as far as effective date of your organization. File Schedule E to determine effective date if you want the effective date to be more than 27 months prior to the application date.

Does the date on Form 1023 meet your organization's needs? If so, do not complete Schedule E. If you need to seek a date prior to 27 months, (for example, you have a donor who needs the tax deduction), then you have to fill out Schedule E and prove to IRS that you meet one of the exceptions to the 27-month filing rules.

Here are the exceptions: Churches, organizations with gross revenue under $5,000 a year, organizations formed before 1969, or if you can prove you acted in good faith and that if IRS granted the earlier date, it would not prejudice the interests of the government. One way you used to be able to prove good faith was to file the Form 1023 before IRS told you to, although it does not always work anymore.

If it is determined that you do not qualify for 501(c) (3) status from date of formation, you may still qualify for 501(c) (4) status for the dates between formation and filing the Form 1023. Normally donations are not deductible for periods covered under 501(c) (4) status.

Line 1: Churches
You only have to fill out Schedule A. Do not complete Schedule E.

Line 2: Gross Receipts
If your gross receipts are under $5,000 or if you are filing within 90 days of the tax year in which your receipts went over $5,000, you get to stop here and not complete the rest of Schedule E.

Lines 3a, 3b, 3c: Group Exemption
If you answer "No," go to line 4. If you answer "Yes," it means you were part of a group exemption application or an actual subordinate of another group that has notified you that you will no longer be part of that group. If this applies, IRS wants to know if you are applying within 27 months of either being turned down or 27 months from no longer being part of the group. If you answer "Yes," you get to stop filling out this form, you are done.

Line 4: Created Before October 9, 1969?
If yes, you get to stop. You are done filling out Schedule E.

Line 5: Why Didn't You File Within 27 Months?
If you answered "No" to lines 1 – 4, answer "yes" to this question. You are not eligible for an earlier 501(c) (3) status effective date unless you can provide an explanation to IRS why you did not file, why you did not file in good faith, and how approving the earlier date does not compromise the best interest of the government. Reasons can include relying on a tax professional's advice that was in error, IRS guidance given in error, complexities in your circumstances making it difficult to ascertain whether to file, etc. You get to stop on this question.

Line 6a: Advanced Ruling
Notice 1382 eliminated advance ruling. Do not answer.

Line 6b: Changes in Source of Support
If you anticipate changes in sources of support, mark "Yes" and fill out line 7.

Line 7: Two Years Projected Income
If you anticipate changes in your source(s) of support, fill out two years projected income using this table.

Line 8: Exemption Under 501(C) (4) For Periods of Operation Prior To Postmark of This Application
If you want to apply for Section 501(c) (4) status for the times of operation prior to the postmark of this application, fill out page 1 of IRS Form 1024 and attach to the application. Although donations will not normally be tax deductible, there will be no IRS taxes due from the organization for the periods covered under Section 501(c) (4).

CHAPTER 31

SCHEDULE F

HOMES FOR THE ELDERLY OR HANDICAPPED AND LOW-INCOME HOUSING

"Winners never quit, and quitters never win."
—VINCE LOMBARDI

If you provide homes for elderly and low-income individuals, you must provide affordable housing to a "significant segment" of elderly, handicapped, or low-income individuals in the community. That doesn't mean you have to have a bunch of houses; it means you have to make whatever housing you have available to a "significant segment" of the people who need it. Don't play favorites or be narrow in focus.

SECTION 1:
GENERAL INFORMATION

Line 1: Type of Housing
Describe the type of housing you are providing (for example apartments, condos, co-ops, private residences).

Line 2: Application
Provide a copy of the application you use to select tenants.

Line 3: Public Awareness
Explain how you advertise your facilities.

Lines 4a, 4b, 4c, and 4d:
Describe each facility, how many people each accommodates, and whether they are renting or purchasing.

Line 5: Contracts and Agreements
Attach samples of documents used for occupancy.

Line 6: Joint Ventures
Provide details of any joint ventures. Make sure the details agree with Part VIII, line 8.

Line 7: Fair Market Value of Services Contracted
Are you contracting with other organizations for services on these properties? If so, how are you arriving at a fair market value for services? Your answer here must agree with Part VIII, line 7a.

Line 8: Management
Elect whether you will manage your facilities in-house, with volunteers, or with independent contractor(s). Make sure your answer agrees with Part VIII, line 7b.

Line 9: Government Housing Programs
Describe any involvement in state, local, and federal government housing programs.

Line 10: Ownership
Do you own or lease? How did you acquire the property? Copies of all applicable documents need to be attached to the application.

SECTION II:
HOMES FOR THE ELDERLY OR HANDICAPPED

Lines 1a and 1b: Who do you provide homes for?
Select which class of individuals (elderly or handicapped or both) you provide housing for. Describe how they qualify and how you select applicants.

Lines 2a, 2b, and 2c: Fees and Affordability
Explain the financial requirements and provide documentation.

Lines 3a and 3b: When Someone Cannot Pay
What do you do when someone cannot pay?

Line 4: Health Care
Do you have health care arrangements for residents? If so, describe them.

Line 5: Needs of Elderly and Handicapped
Describe how your facilities meet physical (such as grab bars in bathrooms, wide doorways for wheelchairs, etc.), emotional, recreational, social, religious, and other needs of the elderly and handicapped.

SECTION III:
LOW-INCOME HOUSING

Line 1: Low-Income Housing
If you provide low-income housing, what is the criteria to qualify and how do you make the final selection?

Line 2: Fees in Addition to Rent Or Mortgage
Are there any other fees? How are they determined? Give a detailed explanation.

Lines 3a and 3b: Is Your Housing Affordable to Low-Income Individuals? Give details and explain restrictions to ensure low income.
IRS gives this guidance at *http://www.irs.gov/pub/irs-tege/rp_1996-32.pdf* Revenue Procedure 96-32, 1996-1 C.B. 717 provides guidelines for providing low-income housing that will be treated as charitable. (At least 75% of the units are occupied by low-income tenants or 40% are occupied by tenants earning not more than 120% of the very low-income levels for the area.)

Line 4: Social Services
Do you provide social services to residents? If so, describe the services provided.

CHAPTER 32

SCHEDULE G

SUCCESSORS TO OTHER ORGANIZATIONS

*"Motivation is simple.
You eliminate those who are not motivated."*
—LOU HOLTZ

The main reason for this schedule is to make sure that no private benefit to shareholders or individuals occurs when one organization (the predecessor) is taken over by or converted to another organization, even if the predecessor was not a tax-exempt organization.

Lines 1a and 1b: Previous Organization For-Profit
Was the previous organization a for-profit organization? If so, give the details of how you came to take it over.

Lines 2a, 2b, 2c, 2d, and 2e: Previous Organization Not-For-Profit
Provide all requested details about the previous organization, 501(c) (3) status, and why you took over the organization and its assets. Be detailed and specific.

Line 3: Name, Address, EIN of Previous Organization
Self-explanatory.

Line 4: Who Ran the Previous Organization?
Provide requested information in the table provided. Attach a sheet if necessary to provide complete information.

Line 5: Will Anyone from Previous Organization Be Involved in New Organization?
Provide complete details.

Lines 6a, 6b, and 6c: Assets
If any assets were transferred to the new organization, what were they, how was their worth established, and were there any restrictions on the sale or use of these assets? Include copies of all agreements made.

Line 7: Debt Transfer
Did the new organization take on any debts from the previous organization? If so, give full details.

Line 8: Leases
Provide full disclosure of any lease arrangements the new organization will have for previously-owned equipment with the previous for-profit organization or any of its members, officers, trustees, or directors.

Line 9: Leases
Will the new organization lease any equipment to the previous organization or any of its members, officers, trustees, or directors? Provide full disclosure.

CHAPTER 33

SCHEDULE H

ORGANIZATIONS PROVIDING SCHOLARSHIPS AND OTHER EDUCATIONAL SUPPORT

"A year from now you may wish you had started today."
—Karen Lamb

IRS wants to make sure that any scholarships you give as a tax-exempt organization are fair in terms of nondiscrimination, merit or need, and available to an open-ended group instead of a preselected group. The scholarship is tax-free to the recipient if he or she is a degree-seeking candidate, and uses the funds for educational expenses that include tuition, fees, books, supplies, and equipment for courses. Acceptable educational expenses do not include room, board, travel, research, clerical help, and equipment not required for a course.

SECTION 1:
PUBLIC CHARITIES AND PRIVATE FOUNDATIONS

Lines 1a, 1b, 1c, 1d, 1e, and 1f: Types of Grants and Loans
Provide a full explanation of grants, loans, and scholarships provided. Although several items are requested, the most important item is the application form for your loan or grant. If you do not have one yet, you can find copies online to use as examples to draft one. Answer each part of this question completely.

Line 2: Case Histories
Do you keep complete records of who gets scholarships, grants, loans, etc.? Describe the records you keep. More information is found in Revenue Rulings 56-304, 77-380, and 1977-2 1956-2 C.B. 306. If you do not keep records, you must explain how you will make sure your program meets exempt purposes.

Line 3: Specific Criteria for Eligibility
Who is eligible? What are your criteria?

Line 4a, 4b, 4c, and 4d: Specific Criteria to Select Recipients
How will you select recipients, number of recipients, the amount for each recipient, and any requirements (such as grade point average) the recipients must meet.

Line 5: Procedures
How will you award the grant and make sure the requirements have been met?

Line 6: Selection Committee
Who is on the current selection committee, what are the requirements, and how do you replace selection committee members?

Line 7: Remaining Unbiased
Are family members of your selection committee eligible? If so, how do you remain unbiased in selection? Private foundations are not allowed to award to disqualified persons.

SECTION II:
PRIVATE FOUNDATIONS ONLY

Public charities do not fill out this section. You are done!

PART IV
FORM 1023-EZ

CHAPTER 34

FORM 1023-EZ
STREAMLINED APPLICATION

*"You are what you think.
You are what you go for.
You are what you do!"*

—Bob Richards

On July 1, 2014, IRS added Form 1023-EZ, *Streamlined Application for Recognition of Exemption under Section 501(c)(3) of the Internal Revenue Code*. This new filing is for smaller organizations and is designed to speed up approval and cut the paperwork down to manageable. It must be filed online, the cost is $275, and you must complete the Eligibility Checklist (which is 5 pages long but not difficult). This is great news for small nonprofits because the Form 1023-EZ is only three pages compared to the Form 1023, which is twelve pages, plus fourteen more pages of schedules, and a two-page checklist. Eligibility worksheet is located in the instruction package for Form 1023-EZ. There are many restrictions on the use of this new form, and many types of nonprofits are not eligible.

To be eligible to use the Form 1023-EZ, you must meet ALL these requirements:

1. Have or project less than $50,000 gross receipts for the past three years and projected for the next three years
2. Have less than $250,000 in assets
3. Be formed in the U. S. and have a U. S. mailing address (or U. S. territory)
4. Must not be a successor to, or controlled by, an entity suspended under Section 501(p) terrorist organization
5. Cannot be a limited liability corporation (LLC)
6. Cannot be successor to a for-profit entity
7. Must not have been previously revoked for failing to file Form 990-series tax returns for three years and applying for retroactive reinstatement
8. Must not be a church, convention, or association of churches
9. Must not be a school, college, university, or cooperative service organization for an educational institution
10. Must not be a hospital, medical research organization, or cooperative hospital service organization
11. Must not be a qualified charitable risk pool
12. Must not be a supporting organization to other nonprofits
13. Must not be credit counseling or consumer credit services
14. Cannot invest 5% or more of your total assets in securities or funds that are not publicly traded
15. Must not participate, or intend to participate, in partnerships (including entities treated as partnerships for federal tax purposes) in which you share profits and losses with partners other than section 501(c)(3) organizations
16. Cannot sell carbon credits or carbon offsets
17. Must not be an HMO
18. Cannot engage in Accountable Care Organization (ACO) activities
19. Cannot maintain donor-advised funds

20. Cannot be testing for public safety
21. Must not be a private operating foundation

Here is a rundown of the sections of Form 1023-EZ with comments to help you answer the questions:

PART 1:
IDENTIFICATION OF APPLICANT

The new form combines Part I and Part V of Form 1023 but eliminates many questions. It is much faster to fill out than the long form.

PART II:
ORGANIZATIONAL STRUCTURE

Most organizations will be corporations, and the organizing document is the Articles of Incorporation. You must be able to check the boxes for questions 5, 6, and 7 for approval. If you used the document templates in earlier chapters, you have no problem checking these boxes.

PART III:

Question 1: NTEE Code is a 3-character code that describes your activities. A list of NTEE codes can be found on pages 18 – 20 of the Form 1023-EZ instructions, which are located online at *http://www.irs.gov/pub/irs-pdf/i1023ez.pdf*

Common NTEE codes include:

P80: Services to Promote the Independence of Specific Populations
X20: Christian
A99: Arts, Culture, and Humanities

D20: Animal Protection and Welfare
F20: Alcohol, Drug and Substance Abuse, Dependency Prevention, and Treatment
I72: Prevention of Child Abuse
O50: Youth Development Programs

There are many NTEE codes. Check them out to find the one that best fits your organization. I suggest you stay away from the codes that start with the letter Y. They are mutual benefit organization codes and do not qualify for 501(c) (3) public charity status.

Question 2: Most organizations are charitable. Remember that you are not eligible to use Form 1023-EZ if you are a school or church organization, or test for public safety.

Question 3: You must be able to check the box attesting that you will not violate the rules.

Questions 4 - 11: If you cannot answer all these questions "No," file the long form to avoid delays and follow-up with IRS because they are going to need much more information to approve you, especially if you are working outside the United States.

PART IV:
FOUNDATION CLASSIFICATION

- Check 1a if your organization will get most of its revenues from donations and grants.
- Check 1b if your organization will get most of its revenues from membership fees and program services fees.
- Organizations that qualify under 1c normally file the long form.

PART V:

Box 1: When you check the box, you are saying you did not fail to file intentionally, and that you have made changes to keep it from happening again.

Box 2: You are seeking reinstatement effective the date IRS processes this application instead of the revocation date.

There are three conditions you must meet to use this form for reinstatement: It must be the first time you were revoked, you must have been eligible to file Form 990-N (electronic postcard return) or Form 990-EZ (short form return), and you must file within 15 months of being revoked.

HOW TO FILE FORM 1023-EZ

Go to *www.pay.gov* and register. Enter 1023-EZ in the search box, and complete the form. You can set up a deduction from your bank account or use a credit or debit card to pay the application fee.

Not everyone is eligible to file the Form 1023-EZ and not everyone should that is eligible. If you cannot use the Form 1023-EZ, you will need to use the long form, Form 1023.

PART V
SPECIAL FEATURE
BY GRANT GURU
JUDY HANNA

CHAPTER 35

THE ART OF GRANT WRITING FOR YOUR NONPROFIT
BY GRANT GURU JUDY HANNA

> *"Like the magic of creating a painting, successful grant writing must capture the combination of skill, creativity, passion, and focus. It's an intoxicating combination once you master the ability to skillfully navigate the diverse offerings and hold that first grant award close to your heart."*
>
> —JUDY HANNA

Every grant writer is a novice in the beginning and, as with all adventures, learning how to present your written proposal is key to reaping the coveted benefits. I once was a novice myself, but with years of practice, stepping in mud holes, and dusting myself off after repeated rejections, I grew into the process as a seasoned, successful grant writer with a good track record. I would like to share some common missteps in the grant writing process to help you avoid costly mistakes and enhance your outcomes for funding.

HOW TO AVOID MUD HOLES AND ACHIEVE GREATER REWARDS

FOCUS

Your mission statement is your focus, the driving force for how you will begin your journey to locate available grants. Below, you will find two sample mission statements. Mission statements are always one statement ranging from one line to five lines.

> **MISSION STATEMENT FOR EDUCATION AND ADVOCACY:** To provide accessible, integrated awareness education and advocacy to senior citizens to enhance quality of life, autonomy, health, safety, and economic well-being, thereby empowering them to live on their own terms independently in their own communities with respect, dignity, and equality
>
> **MISSION STATEMENT FOR HUNGER:** To prepare healthy snacks to pack into weekend backpacks for latchkey kids

RESEARCH

Overwhelming might be a fine term to describe the massive number of corporate, state, federal, foundation, and private grant offerings. To provide you with one example, over 86,700 foundations exist in the United States with reported annual funding exceeding $60 billion, or in visual terms, $60,244,456,505. That number represents foundations that offer funding and does not include the massive number of funding outlets granting awardees through state and federal governmental, private, and organizational giving.

So, where do you begin? The step-by-step process below will provide some guidance and a lifeline to keep you afloat and on the right track for funding your projects.

WHO ARE YOU SERVING?

Revisit your mission statement. Who are you helping through your nonprofit? Let's suppose you are helping elderly with critical needs that aren't covered through other avenues, and the small $800 monthly Social Security check barely covers their utilities and medication. Seniors often are forced to choose between buying food or repairing a rusted-out air conditioning unit, so searching for funding to assist them based on critical needs you have noted would broaden the search to include major corporate foundations such as Home Depot Foundation where new air conditioning units can be secured.

WHY DOES YOUR NONPROFIT EXIST?

Before you begin writing any grant, you must have fact-based knowledge regarding the needs of those you intend to serve through your nonprofit. You must assemble your research to effectively explain why your chosen target groups of underserved people need your help, what they need, and why you exist. Some things to consider:

a. Do you have surveys from your target group?
b. Do you have sourced data from your research as to why you need to help?
c. Do you have media articles?
d. Do you have a target radius?
e. How broad is your scope of help?
f. Do you have a reliable number of approximately how many will be served?
g. Do you have a list of ways in which you will help based on the needs?

WHY DO YOU NEED THIS INFORMATION?

One of the most common mud holes stepped in by novice grant writers is caused by a lack of research on the focus, impact, and outcomes you project for your charity. Funding sources will not fund an organization that can't justify their existence with clear and concise proof of specific needs to be addressed.

HOW DO YOU PLAN TO REACH YOUR TARGET AUDIENCE?

a. Do you have a plan of action?
b. Do you have a core group to help with your project?
c. Do you have a network in place to help you reach your goals?
d. Do you have contact information for your target group?
e. How will you conduct your awareness campaign?
f. How will you be contacted for help?
g. Do you have presentation materials that define your focus?
h. Do you have a marketing strategy?
i. How will you publicize any grants you receive?

WHY ARE THE ANSWERS IMPORTANT?

Funding agents want to know that your group is on solid ground with a well-crafted set of tools to ensure that people who need help can contact you. It is important to have a network in place with similar organizations, news media, materials, speaking engagements, and a referral base. All major funding outlets want to know that your commitment to what you propose is worth the honor of handing money over to you.

> IT IS IMPORTANT TO HAVE A NETWORK IN PLACE WITH SIMILAR ORGANIZATIONS, NEWS MEDIA, MATERIALS, SPEAKING ENGAGEMENTS, AND A REFERRAL BASE.

HOW ARE YOU DIFFERENT?

It is important to show a funding source that you are simply not duplicating services already in place for your target group. Prepare information that clearly shows what is available and what is not. By doing this, you assure the funding source that you are not reinventing the wheel, but are instead offering a service that is deficient or fully lacking for your target group. Research every organization or group that offers assistance to your target group, and define the differences or lack of available assistance.

BEING DIFFERENT IS GOOD IN THE GRANT WORLD

Funding sources do not want to fund an organization that is simply a spinoff of another organization with highly similar well-organized methodology.

THE PROCESS BEGINS

Now you can begin the Internet search for available grants. I suggest that grant writers first search what is available in their own state for nonprofits like yours. We go back to our example of helping elderly. Your search should begin with this broad information: "Funding grants for elderly." That search will display page after page of possible grants available to serve the needs of elderly. Then you will need to weed out those grants that do not apply to your mission statement.

Beware of the hype ads that ask you to pay for information. Do not step in that mud hole. There are unscrupulous scammers who constantly push "free" grants but want you to send money for the information you seek. Information for legitimate outlets is available, and if you are willing to take the time to search them out, your only cost to find what you are looking for is your investment of time.

ARE YOU ELIGIBLE?

Every grant listing has criteria attached. A funding source in Oklahoma may only serve needs in Oklahoma, Texas, and New Mexico, so if you are in Tennessee, you will not want to step in another known mud hole and write a grant to a funding source that clearly does not serve your state. Most grants exclude funding for individuals, private organizations (you are a public charity, not a private organization), building projects, operational funds, and fundraisers.

READ THE GRANT CRITERIA

Once you have located available grants that fit the mission of your organization and you are eligible, and then carefully read the criteria for submitting. You will find that some grantors have short windows for applications and will not review if sent outside of the stated open submission dates. Stay within those dates when you submit.

Pay attention to the following instructions you will face:

a. Some grantors have their own form that must be submitted
b. Most grantors provide an outline of information needed from your organization
c. Some grantors require a query letter before submission
d. Some grantors require that your organization carry a $1 million insurance policy
e. Some grantors require your organization to be in operation for two years before submitting a proposal
f. Most major grantors require a recently completed audit before considering a request from your group
g. All grantors require a copy of your nonprofit designation paperwork (determination letter, and sometimes articles of incorporation)

h. Some grantors require that your organization thank them publicly and provide proof of the announcement after a grant is awarded. Publicity is usually via newspaper, magazine or television.
i. Most government sources will post "request for proposals" for various types of offerings and every specific item requested must be addressed according to the guidelines posted for the request. Competition is fierce for government grants and a poorly written or researched grant will be rejected quickly.
j. Foundation and corporate grants often request online-only applications that must be uploaded to the foundation or corporate website. Read the criteria and assemble your information before heading into the application. Copy a set of the listed criteria and take the time to handwrite your responses and refine the information before inputting information into the actual application form.
k. Some outlets will only fund if you will allow them to see your books first.
l. Local funding sources are user-friendly and less intense on criteria, but only small amounts are generally provided to awardees.

CAPTIVATE YOUR FUNDING SOURCE

Capture the reader's attention immediately when writing a grant proposal. You hold the power to ensure that the grant source sees your heart and feels your determination. The grant proposal is your executive summary of sorts that grabs the interest and attention of the reader. It is your chance to compel the reader to continue reading. The passion, the brief data, and the strength of your plan will be highly evident when you define and explore the depth of the needs you will fulfill. A weak start is often a quick turn off, and your grant proposal joins thousands of other proposals in File 13 without a backward glance.

A PICTURE IS WORTH A THOUSAND WORDS

Providing a picture within your grant request is powerful. Visual learners inhabit the planet and are drawn to consume the meaning of photos incorporated in grants. If you are helping battered women, photos of battered women you know (with permission) are powerful. If you are helping provide backpacks with healthy food for children, the photos of children with the backpacks and the type of food you provide are compelling.

Document every activity you have within your organization with photos. They will come in handy when you decide to submit a grant request. Showing a funding source what you have done is one of the greatest tools you will bring to the table to substantiate your request and achieve higher attention levels for funding. Don't overdo it. Choose your photos with care, and don't utilize a large number of photos.

FOLLOW INSTRUCTIONS

The biggest mud hole in existence for grant writers is not following the instructions provided by the grantor. Read and reread every stated requirement for submission. Check and double-check your materials for compliance. If the grant source requires a cover letter and you fail to include one, it's over. A forgotten financial report, a summary that does not meet length requirements, or failure to include your website address are reasons for disqualification. Competition for grant money is fierce, and one small mistake will take you out of the running.

LANDING SMALL GRANTS VS. LARGE GRANTS

Smaller grants tend to be easier to secure, so don't dismiss the possibility of writing numerous small grants to businesses and corporations. Many small grant awards can add up quickly. Don't dismiss writing small one-page request grants to service organizations in your area. Those add up as well and generally range from $250-$1,000 per grant. Smaller grants do not normally require the intensive work that must go into larger grants. A federal or state grant may take more than two full months to write, but if you are focused on the process and have your ducks in a row, the payout can be massive. There are never guarantees that you will receive one thin dime from your efforts. The rejection letters can leave you feeling depressed and frustrated, especially when you worked so hard to craft a heartfelt submission. It's like anything you do in life; practice makes perfect. Try and try again because different readers with different perspectives are reviewing your work and request. A failed grant from one funding source may even pass muster with another.

AUTHOR'S NOTE

I have worked with Judy Hanna and she is one of the best grant writers I have ever known. She has seen great success as a large grant writer and presenter for over 25 years, provides custom designed grant writing workshops for groups, organizations, colleges, universities, and schools across the United States upon request, and provides grant writing services. If you are looking for a talented grant writer, look no further. She doesn't know I am including this, but for further information and quotes, email *hannajudy@icloud.com*

PART VI
SPECIAL CIRCUMSTANCES

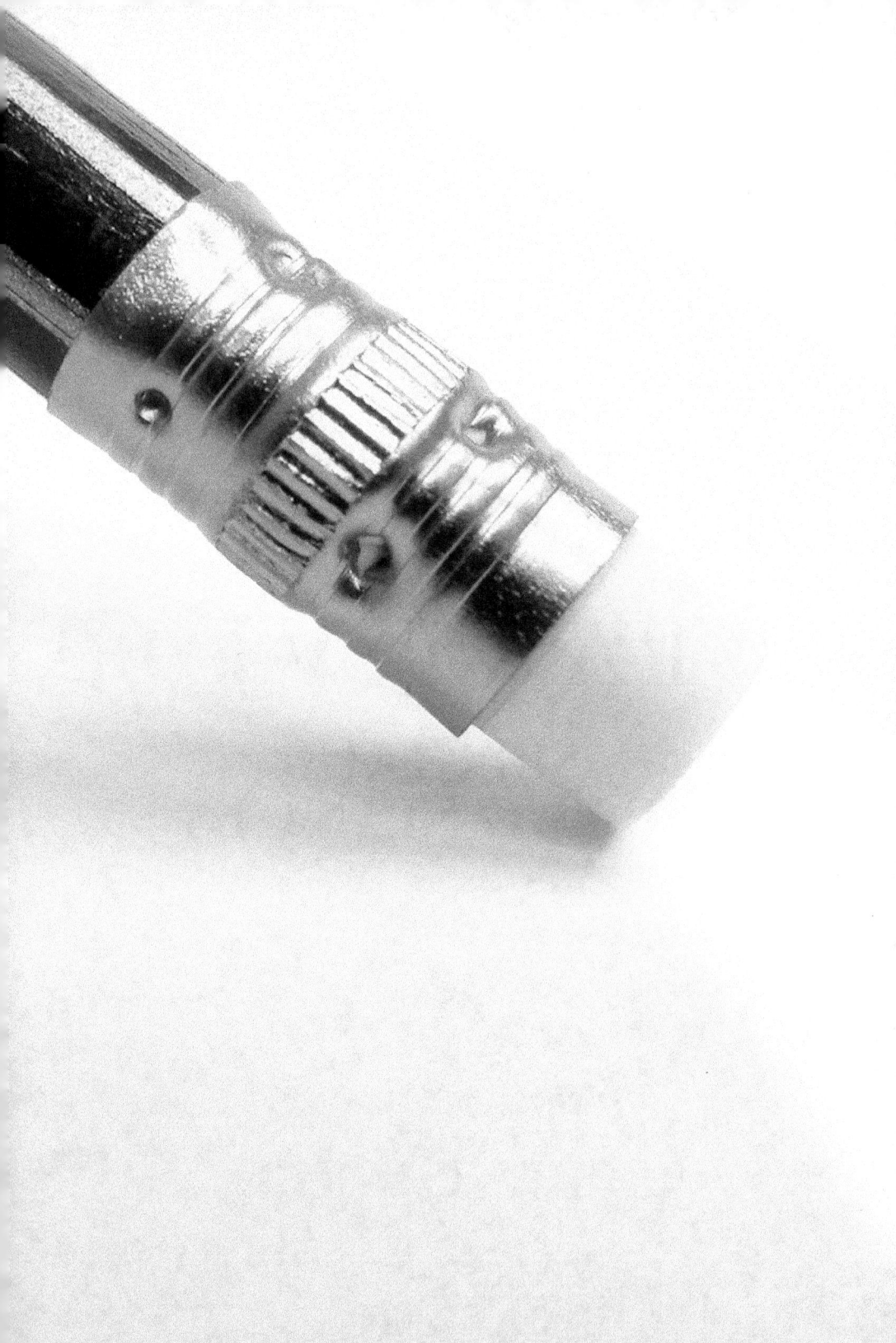

CHAPTER 36

AUTOMATIC REVOCATION OF 501(C)(3) STATUS

"Confidence doesn't come out of nowhere. It's a result of something ... hours and days and weeks and years of constant work and dedication."

—ROGER STAUBACH

Most tax-exempt organizations have to file an annual report with IRS. This report is some version of Form 990, and can be:

- Form 990, Return of Organization Exempt From Income Tax
- Form 990-EZ, Short Return of Organization Exempt From Income Tax
- Form 990-PF, Return of Private Foundation
- Form 990-N, Information e-Postcard

If you fail to file this return for three consecutive years, IRS takes away or revokes your tax-exempt status. This is called *Automatic Revocation* because the computer does it automatically and you are put on a list of organizations that no longer have tax-exempt status. That list can be found at *http://www.irs.gov/Charities-&-Nonprofits/Automatic-Revocation-of-Exemption-List*

If you have been automatically revoked, you must resubmit your entire application (including the required fee) and ask IRS to reinstate your tax-exempt status.

BE SURE TO WRITE "AUTOMATICALLY REVOKED" AT THE TOP OF THE APPLICATION AND ON THE ENVELOPE.

Details of the reinstatement process are contained in IRS Notice 2011-44 located at *http://www.irs.gov/irb/2011-25_IRB/ar10.html*

Normally the reinstatement date is the date of the new application to IRS, but there are some exceptions. For the date to be retroactive back to the date of revocation, you must file your application for reinstatement within 15 months of whichever is later:

- The date on the revocation letter from IRS
- The date IRS posted the revocation on their website

In addition, you have to jump through some hoops to get the retroactive date. For example, IRS requires you to submit a request for retroactive reinstatement attached to the Form 1023 that includes:

- A detailed statement of all the facts surrounding repeated failure to file for the entire three-year period as well as for each individual year.
- What circumstances led to continual failure, discovery of failure, and what you did to stop or lessen the consequences of the failure to file.
- You must address what you are doing now to keep this from happening again. You can add the task of filing the appropriate return to the job description of one of the board positions such as secretary or treasurer to make sure it gets done and that there is a responsible person to carry out the task or follow up with a

bookkeeper or accountant to see that it is done and filed on time in the future.
- Documentation and evidence of the explanations you gave to get retroactive reinstatement.
- All the missing returns for all the years a return was due (some form of Form 990), including the three years not filed and the current year if applicable. If in doubt, contact IRS and ask them specifically what returns are due.
- A signed and dated statement from an authorized official (trustee, officer, or director) that says:

I, (Name), (Title) declare, under penalties of perjury, that I am authorized to sign this request for retroactive reinstatement on behalf of [Name of Organization], and I further declare that I have examined this request for retroactive reinstatement, including the written explanation of all the facts and information pertaining to the claim for reasonable cause and the evidence to substantiate the claim for reasonable cause, and to the best of my knowledge and belief, this request is true, correct, and complete.

- You must provide proof that you "exercised ordinary business care and prudence in determining and attempting to comply with… reporting requirements under section 6033 for each of the three years, and over the entire three-year period." IRS will consider all your evidence and determine if you meet the Reasonable Cause Standard. Here are some things they consider that can lead to a favorable decision:

    a. If you relied on written information from IRS that was in error
    b. Events beyond your control that caused you not to be able to file for each of the three years and the three-year period as a whole
    c. Acting responsibly by taking steps to avoid the failure to file and to keep it from happening in the future by trying to

prevent the failure if it was foreseen; removing the problem that caused you not to file as soon as you became aware of the failure to file; putting policies and safeguards in place to make sure it doesn't happen in the future

d. A history of complying with filing and other requirements before and after the three-year period

e. How heavily you rely on volunteers to perform organizational activities also plays a part in the decision-making process. The more volunteers, the easier IRS will be on you about getting reinstated.

If you want retroactive coverage of tax-exempt status, you need to be very thorough in your explanation of what happened and make sure you let IRS know that you did not fail to comply as a rebellion against the tax system. You may even want to start your explanation with that statement so IRS gets the idea immediately that you were not rebellious. You must provide evidence of everything you say to justify the problem, and you must make sure you have instituted safeguards to make sure it never happens again. If your request for retroactive status is turned down, the date of your new Form 1023 filing will be the effective date for tax-exempt status.

You will not be revoked a second time unless you fail to file for three years AFTER receiving the new determination letter reinstating your tax-exempt status.

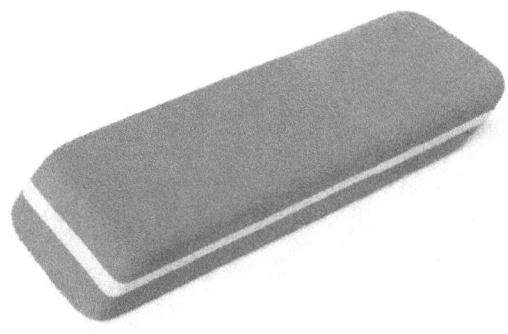

PART VII
FOLLOW-UP TASKS

CHAPTER 37

ANNUAL FILING REQUIREMENTS WITH IRS

"It's not the size of the dog in the fight, but the size of the fight in the dog."

—ARCHIE GRIFFIN

> **IMPORTANT RULE:** If you are a nonprofit, you must file an annual tax return even if you have not applied for 501(c) (3) status yet. The requirement is based on your organization having state nonprofit status, not on IRS granting 501(c) (3) status. Churches do not have to file annual returns.

The IRS gives you tax-exempt status, but with conditions. You must report to them annually (with very limited exceptions) about the income and expenses of the nonprofit organization. The form used to report depends on the status of the organization in terms of revenue, assets, and type of nonprofit. The smaller you are, the less you have to report. In most cases, if your income is less than $50,000, you do not even have to give an exact amount.

If you are a church or subordinate auxiliary of a church, you have no reporting requirements. However, many churches choose to report voluntarily to create transparency and keep everything on the up and up. Other organizations that do not have to file annual reports include state institutions and organizations that fall under parent organizations and qualify as auxiliary organizations of the parent. When in doubt, call IRS and ask. The number is 877-829-5500.

If you fail to file the required form for three years, your tax-exempt status will be automatically revoked the third year. At that time, you must reapply for tax-exempt status and pay the fee all over again, except that you must justify the reason for not filing (for each year you didn't file and for the entire time of failure to file). Consider assigning the responsibility of completing the required returns to a specific position on the board of directors or board of trustees so that it gets done on time every year. The person holding the assigned position should be responsible for reporting the progress, the completion, or problems to the board concerning the required filings. Being assigned to make sure it gets done is not the same as having to actually do the paperwork. An accountant or bookkeeper can do the return. It is the assigned board member's job to make sure it gets done and filed on time.

> IF YOU FAIL TO FILE THE REQUIRED FORM FOR THREE YEARS, YOUR TAX-EXEMPT STATUS WILL BE AUTOMATICALLY REVOKED THE THIRD YEAR.

The reports you file with IRS are public records except that the name of the donors and the amount of their contributions are not public record. When filing, leave off social security numbers and other identifying information for the officers, directors, trustees, and other officials because the information given in the return is available to the public.

Filing a nonprofit tax return consists of completing some version of the IRS Form 990. The versions are similar to the Form 1040 that individual taxpayers file in that there is a long form (Form 1040), short form (Form 1040A), and the simple, uncomplicated form (Form

1040EZ). The difference is that the Form 990 series is for nonprofits and there is no tax due; the filing is for information only. You can look at the various Forms 990 and review the required information at *http:// www.irs.gov/uac/Current-Form-990-Series-Forms-and-Instructions.*

The available versions for tax-exempt organizations are:

FORM 990
RETURN OF ORGANIZATION EXEMPT FROM INCOME TAX

This is the long form that must be filed if an organization's assets are over $500,000 or their annual revenue from all sources is over $200,000. It applies to all Section 501(c), 527, or 4947(a) (1) organizations except black lung benefit trusts and private foundations. The long form is similar to a tax return for an individual with a business. Just like an individual tax return, not everything on the form applies to everyone filing the return. Also, depending on the nature of the business, extra schedules may be required. A nonprofit organization may be required to file extra schedules depending on the nature of the nonprofit endeavors, interaction with other organizations, types of fundraising, political activity, compensation, operations outside the United States, and other considerations.

FORM 990-EZ
SHORT FORM RETURN OF ORGANIZATION EXEMPT FROM INCOME TAX

This is the short form that may be filed if an organization's assets are under $500,000 and their income is less than $200,000. The exceptions are sponsoring organizations of donor-advised funds, organizations that operate one or more hospital facilities, and certain controlling organizations defined in Section 512(b) (13). They must file Form 990.

FORM 990-N
E-POSTCARD

Most smaller organizations with 501(c) (3) tax-exempt approval and income under $50,000 can file the Form 990-N, but can also file the Form 990-EZ or Form 990 if desired. To file, go to *www.irs.gov* and search for Form 990-N. This return is very easy to complete and requires only a few pieces of information: legal name (and any other names used) and address of organization, employer ID number, tax year, name and address of a principal officer, website address if you have one, confirmation that income is less than $50,000, and notification in the case that an organization is going out of business.

This return does not require divulging the income of the organization, except that it is under $50,000. The e-postcard can be completed and filing done in less than 10 minutes per year. With such a minimal effort required for small organizations to stay IRS-compliant, there are few good reasons to be revoked for not filing every year.

FORM 990-PF
RETURN OF PRIVATE FOUNDATION

Section 4947(a) (1) trusts are treated as private foundations. Private foundations are not the focus of this book.

WHERE TO FILE

If you need help with filling out the forms or figuring out which form to file, you can call IRS at 1-877-829-5500.

For organizations within the United States, returns are normally sent to:

Department of the Treasury
Internal Revenue Service Center
Ogden, UT 84201-0027

For organizations with a principal business office outside the United States, returns are normally sent to:

> Internal Revenue Service Center
> P.O. Box 409101
> Ogden, UT 84409

WHEN TO FILE

The filing deadline with IRS depends on the fiscal year of the organization. Filing due date is 4 ½ months after the fiscal year end. There is an extension possible, just like for individual income tax returns. File IRS Form 8868 to get a six-month extension. IRS will mail you a confirmation letter that your extension is approved, but it may take 6 – 8 weeks to arrive.

If an organization's fiscal year ends December 31, their Form 990, 990-EZ, 990-PF, or 990-N is due by May 15th of the following year. The extension for Form 990, 990-EZ, or 990-PF is until November 15th. No extensions are given for Form 990-N. To get an extension for 990, 990-EZ, or 990-PF, you must file IRS Form 8868, *Request for Extension of Time to File an Exempt Organization Return*.

CHAPTER 38

APPLY FOR NONPROFIT STANDARD MAIL RATES

"To succeed you need to find something to hold on to, something to motivate you, something to inspire you."

—Tony Dorsett

Once you have nonprofit status with IRS, you may be able to get a nonprofit standard mail rate with the United States Postal Service. Eligible nonprofit organizations include religious, educational, scientific, philanthropic (charitable), agricultural, labor, veterans, and fraternal.

A responsible official from your organization must fill out United States Postal Service (USPS) PS Form 3624, *Application to Mail at Nonprofit Standard Mailing Rates*. You can get the form online, or you can get a copy of it at the post office. There will be some documents required to submit with the application. More information is contained in USPS Publication 417. You can view a copy online at *http://pe.usps.gov/text/pub417/welcome.htm*

Taking the time to get approved for nonprofit mailings can save a bunch on postage. The post office will weigh one item in your bundle of exact mailings and multiply by the number of items you are mailing. The rate is lower if you use a barcode on your mailing pieces and if they can be processed by machine instead of by hand. Talk with the post office about how to secure your newsletters or other mail pieces.

If you use staples to close a newsletter, your newsletters get torn in processing and can prohibit machining the mailing. Tape and postal seals work better and save on postage because they can be processed as machinable mail, saving significantly on every item.

It's best to talk with the postal workers who will actually process your nonprofit mailings before you send any out. They can give you all the discount information and all the requirements, so you get your mailing ready correctly the first time, and they can show you examples of properly prepared bulk nonprofit mailings. Visit your local post office and ask to talk with someone who handles nonprofit bulk mailings.

SUMMARY

"Never engage in a battle of wits with an unarmed person."
—Dr. Kitty Bickford

I hope this book has helped you navigate the often-tricky waters of government procedure and bureaucracy at state and federal levels. These rules and requirements exist to safeguard the public from fraud and scams, but for those of us who are hardworking, honest people, it may seem like overkill. Granted, applying for 501(c)(3) may not have been the easiest thing you ever did, but think about the result and the good you will do in the future because you completed the process now. I think you will agree it was worth the effort!

I have tried to make the whole 501(c)(3) process simple from idea to reality by providing step-by-step guidance. I am also willing to answer specific questions for you as you go through the process. Please feel free to contact me at any time for additional help. You might also want to visit my websites at *www.taxexempt501c.com* or *www.doyourownnonprofit.com*

May God richly bless your efforts!

APPENDIX A

ACTUAL APPROVED NONPROFIT APPLICATIONS

DON'T REINVENT THE WHEEL!

One of the best parts of starting a nonprofit corporation is that you do not have to reinvent the wheel. If you know of a similar organization, you can request a copy of their Form 1023 with narrative. Wording on applications is not copyrighted, and if you see something you can use, tweak it to fit your organization instead of starting from scratch. Don't make it any harder than necessary.

I have included links to many approved nonprofit applications to help you get through the process. If you see one in this list that's similar to your organization, go to the website and review the application. All links worked at the time of publication.

Some packages given are Forms 1023 prior to the 2013 revision of the form (the 2006 form was almost identical), but the information is similar. Applications that contain the narratives are very helpful in understanding the kinds of information IRS wants to know to approve your application. I included a variety of nonprofits in the list to give you a wide assortment to choose from.

The budget information in the applications below ranges from $0 for brand new nonprofits just starting, up to budgets of hundreds of thousands of dollars or more. These are included to give you a broad range of examples. In addition, many also include their organizing documents and bylaws. Those organizational documents that contain the determination letter or other correspondence from IRS have been added after IRS completed their application. Your paperwork will not have those until IRS sends them after the fact.

West Hill Community Association:
http://mywesthill.org/wp-content/uploads/2015/06/WHCA-501c3-Application.pdf

Chive Charities:
https://chivecharities.org/uploads/pdfs/Form_1023.pdf

The Cannon Beach Academy:
http://thecannonbeachacademy.org/docs/1023.pdf

The Reno Initiative for Shelter and Equality
http://www.renoinitiative.org/wp-content/uploads/2014/03/FORM1023_3.1.13.pdf

Calapooia Food Alliance (Narrative only):
http://calapooiafoodalliance.org/papers/1023%20documents/Calapooia%20Food%20Alliance%201023%20attachment%205-01-09.pdf

Trek Continues, Inc.:
http://www.duffylaw.org/tcaa.pdf

LegalCORPS:
http://legalcorps.org/wp-content/uploads/2012/01/1023-PubInspCopy.pdf

Friends of the Trumbull High School Choir, Inc.:
http://www.fothsci.org/uploads/5/2/4/9/5249683/fothsci_form_1023_application_for_recognition_of_exemption_-_501c3.pdf

The HAMS Harm Reduction Network, Incorporated:
http://hamsnetwork.org/corporate/f1023.pdf

Friends of Niger:
http://www.friendsofniger.org/pdf/FONTaxExemptApp.pdf

Global Literacy Project, Inc.:
http://www.glpinc.org/IRS_Filings/GLP_501(c)(3)_Application-IRS_Form_1023.pdf

Minnesota Groundwater Association Foundation:
http://www.mgwa.org/foundation/documents/mgwaf-irs-1023.pdf

United Way of Metropolitan Chicago:
http://uw-mc.org/wp-content/uploads/2008/11/UWMC-IRS-Exemption-Application-1023.pdf

The Clear Fund:
http://www.givewell.org/files/ClearFund/Clear%20Fund%20Form%201023.pdf

Equipped to Survive Foundation, Inc.:
http://www.equipped.com/etsfi_form1023.pdf

The Light Millennium, Inc.:
http://www.lightmillennium.org/501_c_3/lmtv_form_1023.pdf

Wycliffe Bible Translators International, Inc.:
http://resources.wycliffe.net/financials/WBTI_1023_Application.PDF

Software Freedom Conservancy, Inc.:
http://sfconservancy.org/docs/conservancy_Form-1023.pdf

Rocky Mountain Foundation of Hope:
http://www.rockymountainhope.org/_wp/wp-content/uploads/2010/01/RMFH%20Form%201023.pdf

Arizona Center for Investigative Journalism, Inc.:
http://arizonawatch.org/wp-content/uploads/2012/08/Final-1023.pdf

A Grain of Hope Foundation, Inc.:
http://www.agrainofhope.org/form1023.shtml

Your Town Alabama, Inc.:
http://www.yourtownalabama.com/wp-content/uploads/2013/07/IRS-1023-Application-for-Recognition-of-Exemption.pdf

Playa del Fuego, Inc.:
http://playadelfuego.org/sites/default/files/boddocs/IRS-1023-complete.pdf

Other Applications that give a wider range of nonprofit examples:
The Creek Bed Foundation, a Charitable Trust:
http://thecreekbedfoundation.org/CreekBed1023.pdf

San Diego Speculative Fiction Society, Inc.:
http://www.sansfis.org/corporate_documents/IRS-1023/sansfis_irs1023.pdf

National Consortium for College Completion, Inc.:
http://www.completecollege.org/docs/Form%201023.pdf

Husky Swimming Foundation
(Also shows good wording to expedite application):
http://www.huskyswimmingfoundation.com/wp-content/HSF_Form1023.pdf

Shoe Giver of Tampa, Inc.:
http://shoegiveroftampa.org/pdfs/Shoe-Giver-Application.pdf

The Cordoba Initiative:
http://www.investigativeproject.org/documents/misc/435.pdf

Blount County Humane Society:
http://www.blountcountyhumanesociety.org/PDFs/BCHS%201023.pdf

Gaskov Clerge Foundation (GCF):
http://www.gaskov.org/Documents/Completed%20
990%20Forms/GCF501C3%20%20%20501c3.pdf

Society of King Charles the Martyr, Inc.:
http://www.skcm-usa.org/Legal/SKCMForm1023asFiled.pdf

Vial of Life Project:
http://www.vialoflife.com/images/Application%20for%20501-c-3.pdf

Grandfather Mountain Stewardship Foundation, Inc.:
http://www.grandfather.com/wp-content/uploads/2011/06/
Application-for-Recognition-of-Exemption-Under-Section-501c3.pdf

Continuation Fund, Inc.:
http://antiochcollege.org/sites/default/files/docs/
Continuation_Fund-1023_Applicatio.pdf

Rural Investment Corporation:
http://www.cfra.org/sites/www.cfra.org/files/RIC_
Application_for_Recognition_of_Exemption_1023.pdf

Mozilla Foundation:
http://static.mozilla.com/foundation/documents/
mf-irs-501c3-application-form-1023.pdf

The Jackson Foundation:
http://www.thejacksonfoundation.org/Form1023.pdf

Cadasil Together We Have Hope Nonprofit Organization:
http://cadasilfoundation.net/1023%20Original%20
%20Application%20for%20Website.pdf

Dianetics Foundation International:
http://www.xenu-directory.net/documents/
corporate/irs/1993-1023-dfi.pdf

Wayland Public Schools Parent Teacher Organization, Inc.:
http://waylandpto.org/wp-content/uploads/2012/08/Form-1023.pdf

Multiple Sclerosis Foundation, Inc.:
http://990online.com/docs/5/592792934_87_1023.pdf

CAIRN Rescue USA:
http://www.cairnrescueusa.com/docs/CRUSA_1023.pdf

Quixote Humane Incorporated:
http://www.quixotehumane.org/501c3/
Quixote_Humane_Form_1023.pdf

United States Australian Football League, Inc.:
https://usafl.com/files/USAFL%20Form%20
1023%20Exemption%20Application.PDF

Austin Browncoats:
http://www.austinbrowncoats.com/docs/ABC_1023.pdf

Trinity Mission Works, Inc.:
http://www.trinitymissionworks.org/
Documents/IRS%201023%20ap.pdf

Moldova Mosaic Foundation:
http://moldovamosaic.org/mmorg/wp-content/
uploads/2011/02/Form-1023-web.pdf

Older but good fundraising explanation:
Nautilus of America, Inc.:
http://oldsite.nautilus.org/admin/taxform-1023.PDF

No Form 1023, but good Narrative section worthy of including:
San Francisco-Krakow Cities Association:
http://www.polishclubsf.org/Summary.pdf

Note from the Publisher

Are you a first time author?

Not sure how to proceed to get your book published?
Want to keep all your rights and all your royalties?
Want it to look as good as a Top 10 publisher?
Need help with editing, layout, cover design?
Want it out there selling in 90 days or less?

Visit our website for some exciting new options!

www.chalfant-eckert-publishing.com

www.ingramcontent.com/pod-product-compliance
Lightning Source LLC
Chambersburg PA
CBHW070048080526
44586CB00013B/963